George F. Root

# The Musical Curriculum

For solid and symmetrical acquirement in piano-forte playing, singing and harmony;

containing copious and carefully progressive exercises, pieces, songs, technic

George F. Root

**The Musical Curriculum**
*For solid and symmetrical acquirement in piano-forte playing, singing and harmony;
containing copious and carefully progressive exercises, pieces, songs, technic*

ISBN/EAN: 9783744794107

Printed in Europe, USA, Canada, Australia, Japan

Cover: Foto ©Thomas Meinert / pixelio.de

More available books at **www.hansebooks.com**

# MUSICAL CURRICULUM:

FOR SOLO AND SYMMETRICAL ACQUIREMENT IN

## PIANO-FORTE PLAYING, SINGING, AND HARMONY;

CONTAINING COPIOUS AND CAREFULLY

## PROGRESSIVE EXERCISES, PIECES, SONGS, TECHNICS, SOLFEGGIOS, AND ETUDES,

### IN ALL THE KEYS.

IN WHICH ARE STUDIED AND PRACTICED

CHORDS AND THEIR PROGRESSIONS, TRANSPOSITION, MODULATION AND ACCOMPANYING.

TO WHICH ARE PREFIXED

A METHOD OF TEACHING AND A GLOSSARY OF MUSICAL TERMS AND SIGNS.

## BY GEO. F. ROOT.

———————— •❖• ————————

### CHICAGO:

PUBLISHED BY ROOT & CADY.

1865.

# PREFACE.

TO PARENTS AND GUARDIANS:

My preface will consist of a few plain words to those who have charge of the musical education of others, and who employ teachers and purchase instruments, music and musical books. And first with regard to instruments. It is a mistake to suppose that some worn out or cheap affair will "do to begin with," for saying nothing about the musical enjoyment of player and listeners, strength and flexibility of fingers, and all the other things of execution depend upon practicing upon an instrument that has a *good action*, and the musical perceptions, together with expression and all other things of taste, depend upon having one that has a *good quality* of tone, and that can be easily kept in tune.

With regard to a teacher, it is not always the one that can perform the best that can teach the best, though all other things being equal, the one who can give a good musical example is to be preferred. But having secured a competent teacher, one who has the best interests of his pupils at heart, it is very unwise to bring such a pressure to bear upon him as will force him out of the course he knows to be best for the pupil, in order to gratify any love of display either in the concert room or parlor. It is not unreasonable that you should desire to enjoy as soon as possible the fruits of your expenditure and the labor of the pupil, and it is one object of this Curriculum to provide the means of doing so to a reasonable extent in a legitimate way.

With regard to time for practice, it should not be when the pupil is exhausted with other studies or duties. Overworked people, young or old, can do nothing well, and it is probably better not to undertake the systematic study of music unless a sufficient amount of time can be given for practice when the pupil is fresh and vigorous. A prominent fault in this country is that our young people are required to take too many studies and spend too much time in school for their best growth.

With regard to music to be played and sung, that only should be used which is correct and tasteful; and in respect to words, pure and unobjectionable. Sentiments of bad tendency, and that would not be tolerated in speech, sometimes conceal themselves and pass current in song. In instruction books the various lessons, pieces and exercises, instrumental and vocal, should cover ground enough to afford the means for cultivating *all* the powers of the pupil according to their relative importance, not leaving the execution behind the reading and appreciation, nor *vice versa*; not making time and tune all, and leaving taste and good expression out of the question; and more important than all the rest, not cultivating a parrot-like style of performance that ignores all knowledge of keys and harmonies, as well as general musical intelligence.

May I be pardoned in closing for hinting at the importance of learning music rather for the benefit and pleasure it may be to others than to feed and gratify vanity and self-love, since right views and corresponding motives on this subject will go far toward keeping the pupil in the right course and practicing in the right way.

GEO. F. ROOT.

# METHOD OF TEACHING.

~~~⚹⚛☙☜☞~~~

FELLOW TEACHERS:—

We may all learn something from each other if we are rightly interested in our work, on the principle that every teacher has some ways of his own that are either new, or that suggest new things to others when they are known. Believing this, I come before you, without hesitation or apology, to show, as well as these inadequate means (pen, ink, and paper,) will allow, how I would direct and educate the powers of young people in the study of music, and in the use of the piano-forte and voice. It would be wrong in me to claim all the ideas and plans in this book as my own—many of these are from other teachers,* modified and carried out, however, according to the light that I have on this subject; and as a whole will be found new. Certainly no book has ever before undertaken to cover this ground, and I venture to say that few have ever been made with so much labor, it having been written and re-written, arranged and re-arranged, with interpolations, subtractions, and other changes, many times, before it assumed its present order and form. This would not have been the case had I adopted the plan of any other book, and will, I doubt not, be regarded as some excuse for such imperfection as may after all be found in it.

## TWO WAYS OF TEACHING.

There are two ways of teaching; one shorter, and the other longer. The shorter is to tell all things to the pupil, the longer is to have him find out all he can himself,—or, the shorter is to do for the pupil what the longer would have him do for himself. That which is told or done by the teacher is not thus always made known to the pupil; that which he finds out and does himself always is. That which is told or done by the teacher does not tax the powers of the pupil; that which he finds out and does himself, does not tax the powers of the pupil; gives him no exercise, and causes no growth; that which taxes his powers rightly, both strengthens and expands them. That which taxes some of his powers and not others, produces deformity; that which taxes them all according to their need, tends to symmetry. Things that exist in the nature of musical sounds, can be found out by well guided investigation. Things that man has invented, must generally be told. Finding out and doing the things of music is primary in importance. Learning their names, signs, or descriptions, secondary. This method is to show, as well as may be, what the pupil can find out, and what the teacher should tell,—how the teacher should guide and conduct the investigations of the pupil, and what the pupil should do, and how he should do it, to become an intelligent and skilful interpreter of music for the piano-forte and voice. Such things as are adapted to the powers of the pupil should be introduced and acquired by him when they are needed. This plan is adopted here, and it brings in some things early which have usually been late, or omitted entirely, as will be seen.

And now fellow teachers, I ask permission to assume the familiar manner that we should naturally have, if we were talking together about teaching, because thus I can express myself more clearly on these subjects, which are of so much interest to us all. So I begin by saying: I know, and can do, some things that my pupil does not know, and can not do, but which with the aid of such means as are here, (piano, books, &c.,) and his co-operation, I wish to make him know, and do, and more too, if possible.

## THE BETTER WAY.

Now, which is the better way? Although I have indicated it in general, it will be more clear when brought down to particulars. The first step in every case is to bring that which is to be taught, to the perception of the pupil; and this, according to its nature—that which is to be perceived by the eye, to the eye; that which is to be perceived by the ear, to the ear, &c. Sometimes I would hold it up myself for investigation, and sometimes I would get him to do it; always the latter, when possible. Many things in music that are presented and investigated early in the course, are only learned or acquired after long practise,

* I ought especially to name Dr. C. C. MILLER, of Marengo, Ill., from whom I have received much and important aid.

nevertheless the success of this learning or acquiring, depends upon the right first presentation and investigation. Take for example the first thing named at No. 1, (page 23.)

### POSITION. LETTERS AS NAMES OF TONES.

Shall I present this to the eye of the pupil, or to his ear? This is decided by the nature of the thing—is it a thing seen or heard? If seen, then it must be presented to the eye. This is one of the things that the teacher must present, and I do it by seating myself at the instrument in the right way, while the pupil's attention is called to the position of my body, arms, hands, &c. He does not acquire a good position by seeing me take it; that only comes after some days or weeks of practice on his part, with, perhaps, repeated examples and directions on mine; but the beginning has been made, and it has been made in accordance with the nature of the thing to be acquired.

There are some things of music that are either already known to the pupil, or that are so simple and evident that but a word is necessary to make them known, and for the teaching of which the shorter way, before spoken of, will answer just as well. Such things are, First, that the piano-forte may be made to produce musical sounds, (technically called tones,) and, Second, that these sounds have for their names, the same that are applied to the first seven letters of the alphabet, (with, in some cases, the addition of other words—F sharp, B flat, &c.,) and that these names are also applied to the white keys of the instrument. So I should simply tell the pupil so much of this as he needs to play No. 1. I would tell him no more than where to play C, D, and G, because anything more would be useless at present, and that which is useless, or that which cannot be put into immediate practice, is forgotten soon, and like rubbish, only in the way while it remains. Introducing and explaining only that which can be put right into the work, and thus begin to be incorporated into the musical life of the pupil, is a matter of great importance. At this No. 1, I should let the pupil strike these keys with any finger, and in almost any way, on the principle of having as few difficulties at a time as possible. By way of review I would ask such questions on what has been done as will occasionally be found during the remainder of these remarks on teaching. What is the technical name of a musical sound? How are tones named? How many C's are there on your piano? How many G's? How many D's?

### INTERVALS.

At No. 2, the things to be presented for investigation and subsequent reception into the mind of the pupil, and thence into his action, are intervals. How shall they be presented? As before, of course, according to their nature. Is an interval something to the eye, or to the ear? (Keep in mind that we are speaking of the principal things, not the subordinate things or signs.) To the ear certainly, and must be presented accordingly. By whom?—the teacher or the pupil? The pupil, if he can, by all means, as the more of his own effort in that which he is learning, the better for him. Will he do it by your telling him to manifest an interval with his voice, or by the instrument? Not unless he has previous knowledge on the subject, for he cannot be supposed to know what the word interval means, as applied to music, since that is an invention of man. Will he succeed any better if you point to the sign of an interval, (two notes or different degrees of the staff,) and ask what its name is? Certainly not, and all because names and signs do not come first in the orderly and right presentation; and this brings us back to the thing itself and its presentation. I should simply ask the pupil to strike any two keys of the piano, one after the other, or together, and call his attention to the difference of highness or lowness between them, (technically called pitch;) and after some listening on his part, would say that that difference is called an interval. I would then ask him to manifest a larger interval; afterward a smaller, and at last the one produced by any two contiguous white keys, and this I would name a second. I would ask him to notice the sound of this second, when both tones are heard together, and also when heard, one after the other. I would then ask him to strike two, (still keeping on the white keys,) skipping over one key. When heard and examined, I would name this interval a third. At the next, viz. striking two keys, between which were two others, he would readily give the name, (fourth,) and proceeding in a similar manner, I would introduce the fifth. These intervals I would have him play all over the piano; first with one hand, then with the other; sometimes upward, and sometimes downward. I would then tell him that he might count seconds, thirds, fourths, and fifths, on his hand; that from the thumb to the first finger might be considered a second, from thumb to second finger a third, from thumb to third finger a fourth, and from thumb to fourth finger a fifth; in short, from any finger or thumb to the next a second, to the next but one a third, to the next but two a fourth, and so on, either one way or the other. I would then ask him to play seconds any where on the piano, with seconds on the hand—that is with the fingers, or thumb and finger that are a second apart—so thirds, fourths, and fifths, by their corresponding fingers, with each hand separately, reckoning the intervals, both upward and downward, all over the instrument, calling attention to their differences, and to the different effect of the same interval when played high or low. All this would be training his musical perceptions, or ear as it is called, which is a part of the work of making an intelligent musician. *What is the highness or lowness of tones called? What is the difference in pitch between any two tones called? How many intervals have we found? What are their names?*

MIDDLE C. STAFF. TREBLE CLEF. QUARTER NOTES. INTERVALS ON STAFF. FINGER MARKS.

At No. 3, I should first ask the pupil to strike the C nearest the middle of the piano with the thumb of the right hand. I should then give its name, (middle C,) and while he holds it, should say as follows: Tones as to their highness or lowness (*pitch*,) are represented by lines and spaces, called together a staff. The five long lines and their spaces do not afford places enough to represent all the tones we want to use, so that lines or spaces are frequently added. Either line or space might be taken to represent middle C, but in this book it will be represented by two places only, viz: the first short line below, and the first short line above. When it is to be represented by the short line below, (technically called the first added line below,) a character called the treble clef is placed on the staff. I would here make a short staff with a pencil on a piece of paper, with added line and clef, thus: 𝄞 I would then point to the added line and say, this 𝄞 stands for middle C. Give it on the piano. I should ———— now say, "the added line tells you exactly *what* sound to make, but does it tell you how *long* to make it?" and thus the necessity for notes would appear. I would now ask him to strike middle C about as fast as the pulse beats, and then would make a few quarter notes on a piece of paper thus: ♩ ♩ ♩ ♩ ♩ and tell him that they stand for about the length of sounds that he has been making, and that they are called quarter notes. He would here be easily led to see that notes alone only show how *long* to make sounds, and that the staff is needed to show which particular sound, or what *pitch* is to be given. After showing that the tone D (next above middle C) is represented by the space just below the first long line, I would have the pupil play it with the first finger, and then go through the lesson in an even and correct way, as indicated by the remarks to the pupil. This being done, I would proceed to say each line and space is called a degree, so there are eleven degrees that are always found with the staff. The first degree is the space below; the second the first line; the third the first space; the fourth the second line, and so on to the eleventh degree, which is the space above. If more degrees are wanted they are made by added lines, and their consequent spaces, which are named first added line, first added space; above or below, as the case may be. I would here have the pupil learn that the degrees of the staff may represent intervals, that is that the difference between a line and the space next to it may stand for a second; between a line and the next line a third; between a line and the next space but one a fourth, and so on; or that the difference between a space and the next line to it stands for a second; between a space and the next space a third, &c. In short, from one degree of the staff to the next is a second; to the next but one a third; to the next but two a fourth, &c.

As our language calls the fingers first, second, third, and fourth, it is

manifestly orderly and proper to indicate them in these lessons, by corresponding figures, and those who look at this not very important matter in the exercise of their common sense, cannot fail to see that it is so. There is no particular reason why a cross should indicate the thumb, but as it is in use, I adopt it, notwithstanding that in extremely rare cases it may be confounded with another musical character. I should endeavor *not* to have the pupil practice a moment with wrong positions or movements. *How many lines has the staff? How many spaces? What is each line and space of the staff called? How many degrees has the staff without the added lines and spaces? What are these degrees used for? or in other words, what does the staff represent? What character is used to make the staff so that the first added line below will represent middle. C? What characters represent the length of tones? What kind of notes are used in the lesson? What intervals? What two degrees of the staff will represent a second? What a third? What a fourth? What a fifth? What figure indicates the first finger in the marks of fingering? What the second? What character the thumb?*

BASE CLEF.

At No. 4, I should say as follows: When it is desirable to make the staff so that the first added line above shall stand for middle C, a character called the base clef is placed upon it. If convenient, I would here illustrate with pencil and paper, thus: ———— I would then say, play the C next below middle C, with 𝄢 the thumb of the left hand; try to strike with the thumb 𝄢 only. This tone is represented by the fifth degree of the staff when the base clef is used, (the second space.) Play the G next below this C with the third finger. This tone is represented by the second degree of the base staff, (first line.) After calling the pupil's attention to the proper interval on the hand, I should have him play the lesson, giving him such directions as are printed over it. And I should not like to leave him until they were well understood and observed. *What clef is used to make the first added line above stand for middle C? What interval is formed in this lesson?* It will be here interesting to observe that if the treble and base staves are put near together, with one added line between them, thus: 𝄢 the added line will answer for either staff, and regarded from either staff, will 𝄢 stand for the very same tone which you may now see an additional reason for naming middle C.

MEASURES. COUNTING. BARS. FIGURES. BRACE.

Before playing No. 5, I would ask the pupil to play No. 3 again, but without looking on the book; and while he played, I would count one, two, one, two, one, two, and so on, repeating the words all through. I would then have him play and count himself, speaking the words promptly and evenly. I would then say, this is what is called measuring music, and the time which is taken for each one, two, is called a measure. It might be a good plan here to manifest measures in other ways, as by motions of the hand, or striking gently with the pencil on a book, or by tapping with the foot upon the floor; speaking at the same time of their advantages or disadvantages, but it is not very important. I would then say, play and count two measures—then four—then eight—all this without looking at the book. I would then point to the lesson and say: signs, or representatives of measures are those sections or spaces of the staff which are made by the little perpendicular lines, and these little lines are called bars, and the two bars at the end of the lesson make a double bar. I would also say that the signs of measures are usually called measures, for the sake of shortness and convenience, just as this, ($100) is called a hundred dollars, instead of the sign of a hundred dollars. However much we may yield to custom or convenience in speaking of the various things of music afterwards, it is a good plan to introduce them and their names according to exact truth, in order that the pupil may have clear and intelligent ideas about them. I should then say that measures consist of parts of measures, to each of which we give a count or beat, and that when measures have two parts they are called double measures, or the music so measured is said to be in double time. There is little or no use in the figures 2 at the commencement of the lesson, since the pupil already knows that the measures contain two fourth or quarter notes each, but as it is the custom to use figures, I print them. For the introduction of the other topic, I should say when the two hands play at the same time, the staves which indicate their parts or music, are connected with a character called a brace, placed at the beginning. If more parts are to be performed together, a larger brace is used. *How is music measured while it is being performed? What are those portions of time called which are occupied by equal groups of counts or beats? What kind of measure has two counts or parts? What are signs of measures? What are those lines called that show where these signs of measures are? What are the figures* $\frac{2}{4}$ *for? What is a brace?*

I would here make a remark to my fellow teachers about the early and thorough study of intervals, and give some reasons for so doing.

The player who depends upon looking at the fingers to strike the right keys, labors under great disadvantages. Aside from the bad appearance he makes bobbing his head about, first looking at his notes, then at one hand, then the other, he is liable to become confused by losing his place on the notes, and thus his time in the music. If, however, his hands can take care of themselves, and his eyes be free to watch the notes, he can not only observe all the notation, but can look a little ahead of where he is playing, and thus be prepared for what is coming. To do this, he must be familiar with *intervals*—not only that he may be able to tell them the instant he sees the notations representing them, but his fingers must be educated to make the proper extension or contraction to reach the keys that produce them, without the aid of his eyes. This is best accomplished by careful training from the very beginning. The pupil must learn to *feel*, rather than *see*, how far apart his fingers are—whether they rest upon contiguous keys, or upon those which are apart, and that in making intervals where the whole hand is moved, he may judge by the amount of motion how far his hand must go, just as he carries it to his mouth, forehead, or eyes, without seeing, and apparently without thought.

### OCTAVES.

Before playing No. 6, I should say, strike middle C with the right hand. Now the C next above middle C. This tone is said to be an octave above middle C. Play an octave above the D next to middle C. Now play middle C with the left hand. Now the G next below it. The seventh degree of the treble staff (third space) represents the octave above middle C, and the first added line above in the base, as you remember, middle C. I would here have the pupil play the lesson carefully, leading him to observe and try to do everything necessary to a good performance of it.

### HALF NOTE. ACCENT. MODERATO.

Before playing No. 7, I should say, give me the tone which is an octave above middle C. Play several of these tones such as would be represented by quarter notes, counting while you play, one, two, one, two, &c. *What part of a measure does each of these tones occupy?* Now give me a tone that will fill the measure, or as long as both counts. Play several of these, counting as before. I should now point to the lesson and say, here is a representation of one of these tones, and it is called a half note. While hearing the pupil practice, I would mould and guide him by directions and questions similar to those printed over the lesson. I would then ask him to play the lesson, giving a little more force to the first part of each measure, and this stress or force I would call accent. With accent begins the study of expression, or the more direct cultivation of the musical taste; and I should try to have it tastefully and well done—not too strong, and above all things not monotonous. *How many kinds of tones as to length have we? What are the names of the notes that represent them?* It is proper here to say that we often use the words quarter notes and half notes as names for the length of tones, for reasons already given. I would now play myself, or hum the melody of the lesson; first too fast, then too slow, and then right; trying to have the pupil see that in the right time the lesson sounds the best. I would then say that it is customary to indicate the movements of music by Italian words, and that "moderäto" (third syllable *ah*) is the word indicating this. The reason why Italian words are taken, is that all nations have got into the habit of using them, and they have become, as it were, a general musical language. So we know what the German or French musician means when he marks his music, which might not be the case if the directions were given in his own language.

### METRONOME MARKS.

An instrument called MAELZEL'S METRONOME, is constructed so as to give exactly as many strokes in a minute as the number, against which the weight is placed, indicates. Thus, when a piece is marked ♩=100, it means that one hundred quarter notes are to be played in a minute, or a quarter note for every beat of the metronome. By this you can tell the exact time that the author wishes his piece to go in.

In the absence of a metronome the following will answer as a substitute. Take a piece of tape about two feet long; and at the distance of $4\frac{5}{8}$ inches from one end, make a mark and number it 160; at $5\frac{3}{16}$ inches from the same end mark 152; at $5\frac{3}{4}$ inches, 144; at $6\frac{1}{4}$ inches, 138; at 7 inches, 132; at $7\frac{5}{8}$ inches, 126; at $8\frac{1}{4}$ inches, 120; at $8\frac{3}{4}$ inches, 115; at $9\frac{1}{2}$ inches, 112; at $10\frac{3}{8}$ inches, 108; at $11\frac{1}{4}$ inches, 104; at $12\frac{1}{4}$ inches, 100; at $13\frac{1}{2}$ inches, 96; at $14\frac{3}{4}$ inches, 92; at $16\frac{1}{4}$ inches, 88; at 18 inches, 84; at 20 inches, 80. Then take a bullet or leaden weight, (the exact size is not important,) split it open, and place the end of the tape from which you first measured in the cleft, and fasten it together, with the end of the tape exactly in the centre of the weight. Then taking hold of the tape at the number that is marked over the piece you are about to play, let the weight swing, and for every beat it makes, you will play one note of the kind placed over the piece; for example, if above the piece you find as here, ♩=104, take hold of the tape at those figures and set it swinging, and each vibration will give you the time of a quarter note. As the pupil cannot swing the weight and play too, it is expected to be used only to get a correct idea of the movement, and to start the counting aright.

### MEZZO. FORTE. TIE.

Before playing No. 8, I would say, strike every white key on the piano that is next above the two black ones. These tones are all named E. Play the E that is next above middle C. Now the E, an octave above that, and you will have the new tone represented in this lesson by the fourth space. Strike it eight times without trying to make it either loud or soft. This degree of strength is called *mezzo*, (pronounced *metzo*,) which is usually abreviated to *m*. When, therefore, you see the letter *m* in music, it signifies that you are to play or sing with medium strength. Now play eight times, loud,—this degree of strength is indicated by the word *forté*, (pronounced *forr-ty*,) or its abbreviation *f*. Now give me a tone two measures or four counts long, (one, two, one, two.) Such a tone is indicated here by two half notes connected by a character called a *tie*. While the pupil is practicing this lesson, I would try with great care to have all the directions and hints printed above it observed and fixed, so that there should be no falling back in my absence, and that leads me to say that it is very important to have the pupil make as much progress in the lesson as possible, while you are present—good habits are then so much better formed, and subsequent practice is so much more easy and pleasant.

### RHYTHMICS. MELODICS. DYNAMICS.

We now have something in the three departments of music, and I should introduce their names simply by saying, all things in music that have to do with the length of sounds, belong to a department called *Rhythmics*, just as in mathematics, all that belongs to the adding of numbers together, comes under the head of addition,—all that relates to the *pitch* of sounds belongs to a department called *Melodics*, and all that relates to the strength or force of sounds to the department of *Dynamics*. *What new things have we in this lesson belonging to Rhythmics? What to Melodics? What degree of the staff represents it? What to Dynamics? What have we learned in previous lessons that belong to Rhythmics? What to Melodics? Have you had anything before in Dynamics?*

### TRIPLE MEASURE. DOTTED HALF NOTE.

Before No. 9, I would play a little upon the piano in triple measure, accenting pretty strongly, and would ask the pupil to count one, two, one, two, as before. He would see that this kind of measuring would not answer, and I would ask him to try one, two, three. Then I would say that much music is written in measures of three parts called *triple measure*, or *triple time*. I would introduce the dotted half note, and the two dotted half notes tied, by asking him to play tones that would fill one of these measures, and then tones that would fill two of them, three counts long, and six counts song respectively. In practicing all these lessons, I would have the accent observed carefully and tastefully, as before mentioned, in addition to the printed hints and directions. *How many kinds of measures have we? What is the first? What is the second? How many parts have they respectively?* You notice the figures at the beginning say three fourths or quarters in a measure.

Before No. 10, it would only be necessary to introduce the new tones, which would be done by asking the pupil to strike every white key just below and just above the three black ones, and give their names and the places of their representation in the staves. *Are the new things of this lesson in Rhythmics, Melodies or Dynamics? . What degree of the treble staff represents F? What degree of the bass staff H? How many kinds of intervals are found in the treble part of this lesson? What are they? How many in the base? What are they?*

RESTS.

Before No. 11, I would first introduce the new tone A in the way I have introduced previous tones, and show its representation in the base, and then would ask the pupil to give me four tones, each filling a measure in triple time, (he may use this new tone if he likes.) I would then ask him to do the same with this difference, viz: take off the finger from the key at the last count or part of each measure, leaving the tone but two counts or beats long. I would then ask him to play a quarter note on the first and last parts of each measure, leaving the middle or second part silent as to the music, and perhaps would arrange other forms, in which he could practice the same thing. I would then tell him that passing over a part of a measure in this way is called *resting*, and characters called *rests* are used to indicate it. I would here point to those in the lesson, and say they are called quarter rests, because each one takes up just as much time as a quarter note would. *How many departments are there in music? What are they? Have we anything new in melodies in this lesson? By what degree of the base staff is A represented? Have we any thing new here in Rhythmics? What do rests indicate? Show me seconds in the lesson; thirds; fourths. Are there any fifths?* You see I fall into the way of speaking of intervals, when I mean representations or signs of intervals. This I think does no harm when the pupil knows what is right, and knows that this is done for brevity and convenience.

LONG AND SHORT LESSONS.

My idea is that an average pupil who is beginning will learn one of these lessons in the ordinary practice of one day,—he can skim over and learn the outside in less time, but I mean so thorough a learning of it, that there shall not be a hesitation nor a mistake—indeed so that it shall sound as though he couldn't make a mistake. Have you ever noticed that some playing sounds all the time as if the player was just going to break down, and you involuntarily draw a breath of relief when he gets safely through? Not only should the outside be thus perfect, but the accent and dynamic expression should be in right places, and tasteful. Names of tones and intervals should constantly occur to the mind, and every position and movement should be as nearly correct as possible. Playing a lesson merely in time and tune, should be at least nearly accomplished before the teacher leaves the first giving of it, and this leads me to the very important matter of

RIGHT AND PROGRESSIVE LESSONS.

Lessons should be adapted to the states of the pupil, in the various stages of his advancement; at first not only easy of execution, but so constructed as to embody and express only simple musical ideas or feelings. You will often find in music that is easy of execution, places that beginners do not like, and ought not to be expected to like, being only understood and appreciated, after considerable culture. Take for example the matter of pedal harmony, which is found in much music for beginners; my experience is that it can only be appreciated and liked by persons who have studied and heard music for years, or at least those who have studied many months. Then these right lessons should be so gradually progressive, that the pupil shall find in each one successively, that only an agreeable and reasonable tax upon his time and powers is required to learn and understand it thoroughly. Let me make two pictures. Number *one*. Note or word from pupil. "I havn't learned my lesson; please excuse me," or, "please do

not come to-day," or if no such note is sent, pupil appears, looking anxious and discouraged—perhaps muttering, "I can't play my lesson I know." Being seated, commences—all goes wrong—no proper conception of the music—so love for it—can neither execute nor understand it—or being energetic and desperate, dashes over it with many faults of omission and commission. Teacher annoyed and perplexed says to himself, "now I must either let this lesson go with the difficulties not half conquered, and so send him on unprepared to meet the next; or I must keep him here until he is utterly disgusted with the whole subject, or, I must give up trying to keep him in the instruction book, and must spend half my time in music stores, selecting what is adapted to his state and attainments. Picture No. *two*. Pupil comes in—is evidently glad to see you,—goes straight to the piano and plays his lesson tastefully and well. He has mastered it completely, and enjoys it thoroughly. You have nearly all the hour for the next lesson, which being adapted to the state of the pupil, is well started before the time is up. If at the house of the pupil, mother or sister comes in, and compliments you on the progress that is being made, and perhaps says that although the lessons are simple, they give a good deal of pleasure, and that there is very little difficulty in having the practice hours observed. I fully believe that these pictures are true, and that number one shows the results of wrong lessons, either in quality or quantity, and number two of right ones.

QUADRUPLE MEASURE. WHOLE NOTE.

At No. 12, I should introduce the tone G, in the way already shown, and should then ask the pupil to give it four times, holding each tone while he counts one, two, three, four, thus making each tone four counts long. This I would say introduces both a new note and a new measure, which I would name. I should now say play four measures of quarter notes, and accent the first and third note in each measure, and let the accent on the first part of the measure be a little stronger than that on the third. This is said to be the natural accent in this kind of time. *What new things have we here in Rhythmics? What in Melodies? Anything new in Dynamics? How many parts has Quadruple measure? What do the figures at the beginning of the lesson show? Could you tell that without those figures? What degree of the treble staff stands for this G? What new interval is here? What kind of note is half as long as a whole note? What kind of note is a quarter as long? What three quarters? How many quarters would be equal in length to a half? How many to a dotted half? How many to a whole? On what part of the measure does the accent in this kind of time?* It would be better for the pupil to play the lesson once or twice before the questions are asked. After introducing the F in the base at No. 13, and hearing the practice of the lesson with reference to position, movement, intervals, &c., I should ask the pupil to play it with equal strength throughout, then with Dynamic variety, by means of Mezzo and Forte, and then decide where the application of these Dynamic degrees would make the lesson sound best. It is hardly necessary to remind you that any practice of the pupil at this time, too fast, with wrong movements of fingers, or wrong positions, with unsteady or drawling counting, keeping one piano key down while striking the next, losing the place by not keeping the eyes upon the book, guessing at the notes, not striving to give the expression best adapted to bring out the full meaning of the music, and in general leaving out, or doing wrong, any of the things which go to make a complete and healthy musical growth, proportionately injures, and retards his success.

PIANO. HALF REST.

At No. 14, I should introduce the new things according to their nature, and have the pupil do them before looking at, and learning their signs. *Have we anything new in Dynamics in this lesson? What does piano mean? What is its abbreviation? What is new here in Melodies? How many parts of the measure does the half rest occupy?*

FIVE FINGER EXERCISES, OR TECHNICS.

After learning No. 15, according to the directions, I should say to the pupil, place the thumb of the right hand on middle C, the first finger will then be over D, the second over E, the third over F, and the fourth over G. Now press them all down firmly—now raise only the thumb, and strike with it about as fast as quarter notes. Now keep all down but the first finger, and strike with that—now all but the second—now the third, now the fourth. Now place the little finger of the left hand on the C one octave below middle C, the thumb will be over G, and the other fingers over D, E, and F. Press them all down; then exercise one at a time as you did with those of the right hand. Do not let any key up but the one you are striking. Try both hands together, keeping the fingers properly curved. Now turn to page 45 and you will find this very exercise; also No. 16, the first five finger exercise, and directions with regard to them. I should not expect the pupil to like technics at first, because they are exercises that embody particular difficulties of execution, in the most concise manner, without any attempt to be tuneful, or in any way musically agreeable; but as the pupil experiences the advantage they certainly will be to his execution, he will become more and more willing to practice them daily, and will at last come to like them. In this holding down exercise, the finger that is striking should be kept going until it begins to be tired—perhaps thirty or forty times—and those that are weakest should receive most attention.

Before playing No. 16, I should say, give me a sound eight counts or two quadruple measures long, and then call attention to the way such tones are represented in this lesson.

At Nos. 17, 18, and 19, the new things are so obvious that the pupil will probably see them himself, excepting, perhaps, the measures in No. 19 that are not full, which I should explain by saying that when a piece *begins* with a part of a measure, it always *ends* with a part of a measure also, and that both of these parts are always equal to a full measure. *In what kind of time or measure is this lesson written?* *With what tone does the treble commence?* *What finger gives it?* (I should ask same of base.) *What degree of the treble staff stands for B?* *What for A?* *What for G?* *What degree of the base staff stands for D?* *What for E?* It might be well here to let the pupil make with a pencil on a piece of paper, the two staves, and write the names of the tones on the lines and spaces that represent their pitch, thus:

Play the treble, (of either of these lessons,) naming the intervals as you make them. Do the same with the base. *With how many parts of a measure does No. 19 commence?* *With how many parts does it close?*

SECTION. REPEAT.

At No. 20, I should simply say that a piece of music is often divided into two or more parts, which are called *sections*, and that when a section is to be played twice, dots are placed at the end of it, and form what is called a *Repeat*. Double bars, or larger single bars usually indicate the sections. *How many sections does No. 20 consist?* *How many measures in each section?* *How is the first measure filled in the treble?* (Ans. By quarter notes.) *The second?* *Third?* *Fourth?*

REVIEWING.

I should have the pupil review in this part of the book about twenty lessons, dropping off old ones as he adds new ones, but keeping about three pages in practice. If the lessons are well learned, this will be neither a long nor disagreeable task. I think for the present about one-eighth of the time allotted to practice, should be given to the daily exercises of technics, and about one-eighth to reviewing. More than this will be required by and by.

PREPARATORY SINGING.

At No. 21, the pupil commences singing—not the study of singing, though it might be well to correct any faults that could be corrected without turning him too much from the main work. The idea of singing thus with the playing, is to tune the voice, and prepare it for the more careful study that comes by and by.

No. 22 is the second of a duet for the piano, and brings forward no new

thing excepting position of the pupil at the instrument, and the term "seconds." All culture in the direction of good taste in the performance of these pieces at this stage of the pupil's progress, will have a most salutary effect on his symmetrical growth.

At No. 23, new tones, new positions, treble clef for left hand, and the term "primo," are the new topics, all of which will be easily introduced and understood. Both parts of these duets are to be practiced in their order, as the other lessons are; then if convenient, together, by two pupils, or, perhaps, by teacher and pupil. Duets help to the appreciation of fuller harmony, and in other ways are beneficial. *Upon what degree of the upper staff is the first note of this lesson placed?* *What is the name of the tone here represented by the second added line above?* *How many octaves above middle C?* *What degree of the staff is the third note upon?* (Ans. First added space above.) *What is the name of the tone that this degree stands for?*

KEY NOTE.

Before playing No. 24, I should play a strain in one part that includes tones enough to give a clear and full idea of *feeling* of the key of C, (you can do this with seven tones, though it takes eight to make a complete scale,) perhaps like this:

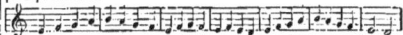

Stopping on some other than the key note. I would then say, does this sound well for a stopping place or ending? Is it a good *home?* If the perceptions of the pupil are so dull that he does not object to D as a stopping place, I would repeat the example in various ways until he does object, for no one can be a musician without perceptions, or as is commonly said, "a musical ear," sufficient for this. When the pupil fully feels that C is the satisfactory resting place or home, I should say that for that reason C is called the key note of such a strain. To make this still more clear, it may be a good plan to play all over the piano, using only the white keys or the tones of the key of C, and still better to let the pupil do it.

F SHARP. KEY NOTE G. SIGNATURE.

I would now ask the pupil to strike the lower black key of each group of three black keys, and after his doing it would tell him that they are all named F sharp. I would then play a strain, using F sharp instead of F, perhaps like this:

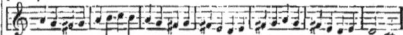

I would then ask if it is the satisfactory resting place note. It is not difficult to lead the pupil from here to find out that G is the *home* or key note, when F sharp is taken instead of F. This presenting the thing itself for the pupil's investigation, makes him *know* it a great deal better than telling him, for example, that when there is one sharp the key note is G; and when there is none, the key note is C. We certainly should endeavor to make our pupils as intelligent as possible about the things they do, or in other words we should make them know as much as we can of the theory, science and art of each, and this is perhaps the most important and distinctive object of this Curriculum. If the pupil should say, why do you have any key note but C?—cannot any tune be played or sung so that the key note will be C? I should reply, some tunes sound a great deal better to be played or sung, so that the key note will be G, and this is the only reason why such tones are sometimes used as make G the key note. The pupil having received this truth, will, when playing or singing in the key of G, have some intelligent idea with regard to the F sharp, and will correct easily the mistakes that he will be sure to make at first, in trying to go to that tone, while looking on his book. I should now teach him that the character called a sharp, placed at the beginning of a piece of music, upon that degree of the staff which lies hitherto stood for F, modifies it, and all other lines or spaces standing for F, so that they now mean F sharp, and that the sharp so placed is called a signature or sign that the key note is G, or as is commonly said, it then becomes the signature of the key of G. Saying that the sharp at the beginning *sharps all the* F's, although afterwards convenient, does not seem to me to be at first so clear a statement. It may be proper here to say that the absence of any character of this kind is said to be the signature of the key of C. If the pupil should discover at this point that there are different kinds of seconds, thirds, &c., and should ask questions about them. I would simply say that there are such differences, but that we do not study about them at present.

*Can we make a satisfactory ending of a piece of music on any tone?* (meaning any tone as to pitch.) *What is the technical name for that tone on which we can stop with the most satisfaction? When only the tones made by the white keys are used, what is the key note? When F sharp is used instead of F in a tune, what is the key note? What is the signature or sign that the key note is G? What does the sharp so placed do? Does it modify any other lines or spaces of the staff? What is the signature to the key of C?* (The answer to this question is usually "natural.") *Does this matter of key note and signature belong to Rhythmics, Melodics, or Dynamics? Is the sharp a Rhythmic, Melodic, or Dynamic character; that is, does it have to do with the length, or the pitch, or the power of sounds? What interval is produced by E and F♯? What by F♯ and G? What by G and A? A and B? B and C?*

### SEXTUPLE MEASURE. DOTTED WHOLE NOTES.

I should introduce these at No. 25, by asking the pupil to give me four tones, each six counts long. he counting while he plays. I would then tell him the name of the measure he had just made, and show him the dotted whole note that stands for a tone six beats long. I would endeavor to lead the pupil to see that the natural accent in this kind of time, falls upon the first and fourth parts of the measure. This can be done, of course, by presenting the thing itself, that is, playing or singing something with those accents rather prominent.

*What new things have we here in Rhythmics? What one note will fill a measure in sextuple time? What two? What other two? What three? What other three? What four? What other four? Still what other four? What five?* (It will be a good plan to have the pupil make other combinations, playing them as he makes them.) *Where does accent naturally fall in this kind of measure?*

At No. 27, we have the metronome mark indicating the time of "audantino." I should, however, explain to the pupil that audantino not only signifies this movement, but also a rather flowing, and never loud or energetic style. The melodies are now beginning to have more meaning, all of which should be developed. For audantino and other musical terms, use the dictionary of musical terms. No new topics to be introduced until we arrive at No. 30, but a far more important work is to be done, viz: learning all the lessons rightly. I suppose we shall all agree that it is a good plan in giving out the new lessons, to take one part at a time, and have the pupil work at the hard places until they are almost within his reach, so to speak, and not leave him until the lesson is so far advanced, that we are sure he will go on in the right way, and with feelings of encouragement, confidence and pleasure. I suppose that we shall also agree with regard to the directions over the lessons that they are useful, and should be kept constantly in the pupil's mind.

At No. 30, we have base clef for upper staff, upon which is the D next above middle C. It seems to me a good plan to have the pupil decide where piano, forte, or mezzo, will make the lesson sound best, as this cultivates his taste and power of expression.

At No. 31, I should explain that "allogretto" not only means the movement indicated by the metronome mark, but a cheerful style. The new tones and positions will easily be explained and understood.

### C SHARP. KEY NOTE D.

At No. 32, I should ask the pupil to strike all the lower black keys of each group of two. These tones I should name C sharp. I should now play a strain of music, making use in it of F♯ and C♯, instead of F and C, perhaps like this:

then say to the pupil "if you do not like this for an ending, end it yourself," which he might do either with the instrument or with his voice. He could hardly fail in this way to find out satisfactorily what the key note to a tune is, when F♯ and C♯ are used, instead of F and C. If all this is done without a book, so much the

better; then turning to the lesson, I would point out the way that the sharps are placed to make the staff represent the key of D, including the fact mentioned before, that every line or space of either staff usually representing F and C, are now made to represent F♯ and C♯, although the sharps are placed on but two of them in each staff. After having the pupil try over the lesson once or twice, I would ask:

*What is the key note of this lesson? What tones are used in it that are not used in the key of C? What are omitted that are used there? What tones make the key of D? What the key of G? What the key of C? What is the signature to the key of D?* (Two sharps.) *What is the signature to the key of G? What to the key of C?*

If the pupil should notice that there are no black keys on the piano between E and F, and B and C, and should ask the reason for it, I should think this as good a place as any to tell him that the tones made by the white keys, although they succeed each other so pleasantly, (I should here illustrate by playing moderately up and down, one or two octaves,) and seem to be so much alike as to the intervals between each two, are in point of fact quite different in this very respect; the interval produced by E and F, and also the one produced by B and C being but half as great as those produced by the other white keys—in fact that they are just like those which are produced by a black key, and the next white one. You notice, fellow teacher, that I *generally tell* the pupil when the things to be learned are so simple or obvious that the investigating and finding out plan, is not necessary. But I *tell* him here for exactly the opposite reason, viz: because this difference in intervals is so hard for the beginner to perceive. If, however, you think differently, you have only to present the subject according to its nature, and let him investigate it.

### STEPS, AND HALF STEPS.

I should add that although there are two kinds of seconds, we do not notice the fact, in speaking of them, but continue to call them all simply seconds, for the present, excepting on certain occasions, when the larger seconds are called *steps*, and the smaller *half steps*. It might be well here to ask the pupil to touch a succession of white keys, naming the intervals as he produces their steps or half steps, then do the same with the black and white. He will notice that from a black key to the next black one in the same group is a *step*, and that from any one to the very next, black or white, is always a *half step*.

*What is the key note of No. 33? What is the signature? In what kind of time is it?*

### MARCATO. CRESCENDO.

At No. 34 I should have the *marcato* effect heard by striking any key of the piano, and then lifting off the finger and hand suddenly. After seeing this done several times in the right way, I should point to the dots under and over some of the notes here, as signs of the marcato, or marked style of playing. I should then have some tone or tones given, beginning piano and gradually increasing to forte, and then, showing the signs of this, we should be ready for the lesson.

At No. 36 I would ask: *What degree of the staff is the first note in the treble placed on?* (Ans. Second added space.) *What is the name of the tune there represented? Does marcato belong to Rhythmics, Melodics, or Dynamics? To which department does the crescendo belong? What should be the name of the rest that is as long as a dotted half note?*

Let me hope that not only these five finger exercises will be learned in their order, but that all the new things will be fairly tested, according to the suggestions that are made with regard to them.

### G SHARP. KEY NOTE A.

At 38, I should introduce the new tone in the way already mentioned; also the new key note.

*What is the signature of this key? What tones are not used in it that are used in the key of C? What tones belong and sound pleasantly here, that are not found in the key of C? What degrees of the treble staff are modified by sharps? What tones do they stand for now?* (Ask same of base.) *How much higher is the tone that one of these sharped lines or spaces stands for, than the tone it stands for when no sharp affects it.* (Now we have an occasion for the word *half step.*)

## DA CAPO. FINE.

At No. 39, I should simply *tell* the pupil that *Da Capo*, or its abbreviation *D. C.*, means go back to the beginning and play to the word *Fine*, which means *finis*, or end. I should endeavor to feel all the time that my great work is not to explain, although that is important in its place, but rather to assist the pupil *to do*, intelligently and thoroughly, everything that he undertakes. Beyond explaining the word "allegretto," which may be found in the dictionary of musical terms, the manner of introducing the *new* things has been shown, until we reach No. 45, when I should have him play all the tones named D sharp, and perhaps let him find out for himself that when D♯, G♯, C♯, and F♯ are used, instead of D, G, C, and F, the key note is E.

At No. 48 I should remind the pupil that a curved line connecting two notes on the same degree of the staff is called a tie, and should now tell him that a

### LEGATO MARK

Is just such a line connecting notes on different degrees of the staff, and that it means link the tones closely together. It might be added that when the legato mark connects but two or three notes, it is in good taste to accent the first one of those so connected.

At No. 42 the remark to the pupil says, "Do not throw the hand up at the rests, &c." This, of course, does not mean keep the tones sounding through the rests, but refers to the rather important matter of

### MANNER AT THE PIANO.

It is the experience of every one, that he who excites your sympathies by appearing to labor very hard while playing, or who undergoes various unpleasant contortions of the features at the hard places, who moves his head, body, or arms unnecessarily, or who makes an undulating motion of the wrist, lifting the hand as though the ends of the fingers were sticking to the keys, as well as he who is rigid like a block of stone at the instrument, detracts much by these things from the pleasure and usefulness of his musical performances. I should, therefore, think it a part of my duty to see that the manner of my pupil at the piano is not ostentatious, but natural and graceful.

### FIRST TIME. SECOND TIME.

The pupil will easily see that the first ending, (which consists of two measures, and is marked "first time,") is omitted in the repeat, and the second ending substituted. I should ask questions about key note, signature, time, intervals, &c., at each time. The introduction of the keys of B, F♯ and C♯, would be accomplished according to the plan already made known.

At No. 56 I should show that E♯ and F are produced by the same white key on the instrument; and in No. 58 that B♯ and C are also made by the same key.

At No. 60 we begin at the key of C again; familiarity with intervals will now be still more important to those who wish to become intelligent as well as independent players.

### B FLAT.

Before playing No. 65 I should say, "the tones produced by the black keys (and some of the white ones) are named by the word *flat*, as well as sharp; for example, the tone that is sometimes named A♯, is also sometimes named B flat, and B♭ is required instead of B when we have F for the key note. This I would illustrate, if necessary, by playing what would show the tones of the key of F.

*How many tones named B flat are there on your piano?* (Touch them.) *What is the signature of the key of F?* On what degree of the treble staff is the flat placed in the signature? Does it modify all the other degrees of this staff that usually stand for B? How much does it modify them? Does it make them stand for tones a half step higher or a half step lower? What tone is found in this key that does not belong to the key of C? What tones are in the key of E that do not belong to the key of C? What in the key of B? What in the key of F♯? What in the key of C♯? What is the signature of the key of D♯? What of F♯? B? E? How many degrees of the staff are changed from their original signification, when the signature consists of seven sharps? Are they changed to stand for higher tones* or lower ones? How much higher? (Similar questions might be asked of the keys of C♯, F♯, B, E, &c.) What tones make the key of C? What tones make the key of C♯? (Similar questions might also be asked of the other keys.)

Until we reach No. 60, there has been no extension of the hand to reach a larger interval than a fifth. When the hand has been properly placed, the fingers have been exactly over the keys to be touched. Now, there must be a little extension of the fingers and thumb to make a sixth *on the hand*. The interval of the sixth does not really occur until No. 62, although the extension spoken of is required at 60 and 61.

### EIGHTH NOTES.

At No. 66 I would say, play four measures in double time, and give two tones to each count; (take any pitch.) These tones may be represented by what are called *eighth notes*, (pointing to them in the lesson.)

*Do the new things of this lesson belong to Rhythmics, Melodics, or Dynamics? How many eighth notes occupy one part of a measure? How many would fill a whole measure? How many eighths are equal to one quarter? How many to one-half?*

At No. 69 I should say, that the whole rest (a little block just under the line) not only represents silence as long as a whole note, but is used to fill a measure in any kind of time.

*What degree of the staff is the first note of the treble in No. 71 placed on? What the second? The third? Fourth? &c. What is the movement of the duet? About how fast by the metronome?*

### SYNCOPATION.

Before playing No. 72, I would introduce the new key, by having the pupil strike every black key next below E; then giving its name, and showing that B flat and E flat, instead of B and E, makes B flat the key note. If the pupil should ask, at any time, why certain tones make a key or key note, I would say, "that will be explained by and by," let the fact suffice now." I should then ask the pupil to select any *pitch*, and play four measures, each to consist of quarter, half and quarter notes, just in that order. I would then say that good taste requires that when a tone begins on an unaccented part of a measure, and continues through the accented part it is to be *accented*, and is then called a *syncopated note*, or a *syncopation*. I should then have him play these four measures, in that style.

*Which are the unaccented parts of quadruple measure? What is a tone called that begins on one of these unaccented parts, and continues through an accented? How in such a case should that part of the measure usually unaccented be performed? What is this kind of tone called? To which department of music does Syncopation belong? In which measure does Syncopation occur in this lesson? In which part? Are there Syncopations in the base?* (Be careful to give the *natural* accent in the base, and the syncopated accent in the treble.) At No. 75 I should simply say that

### APPOGGIATURAS

are the signs of short tones frequently introduced into instrumental music, and that each one usually takes its time from the note that follows it. Do not begin the appoggiatura *before* the base note that occurs on the same part of the measure, but let them commence exactly together. I should question the pupil at *every* lesson on all the important things connected with it, in the manner already described. The introduction of the new keys made by tones named with the word "flat," would be done in the way before mentioned, viz: playing the new tones, then showing how they make the key notes, and how to modify the staff so that it will represent them.

### PLAYING BY EAR.

As it is called, is sometimes objected to, but I am inclined to think it an advantage, especially when connected with a regular course of musical study, for it strengthens the memory, and gives more freedom and naturalness to the expression, and last but not least, it delivers the pupil from the bondage of being always obliged to have his "notes" when performing for the pleasure of others.

### VARIETIES OF MEASURE.

At No. 85 I would say, "thus far a quarter note, or the value of a quarter note, has filled each part of a measure, or in more popular language, we have had thus far a quarter note, or its value, to each count." We may adopt any other note for the standard, that is, to represent the tone that fills one part of a measure. In this lesson an eighth note may be said to be the standard, that is, an eighth (or its value) is taken to stand for so much of the music as occupies one of the six parts of the measure, so the figures at the beginning say six-eighths in the measure. It happens in this kind of measure that it is sometimes more convenient to count two than six. It will be in this case, unless the piece is played rather slowly. It may perhaps here be said that this piece could be represented just as well with quarters for standards, but that eighths are used because it is customary, and because in more difficult music there are good reasons for "varieties of measure." As a dotted half note stands for a tone as long as three-quarters, so a dotted quarter stands for a tone as long as three-eighths. Dal Segno says, "to the sign," instead of Da Capo, "to the head," but both end at the word Fine.

*How many kinds of measures are there? How many varieties of each kind could we have?* (Ans. As many as there are kinds of notes.) *What kind and variety of measure would be indicated by the figures* $\frac{2}{2}$*?* (Ans. Double measure, half variety; meaning two half notes, or the value of two half notes in each measure.) *What by* $\frac{2}{4}$*? What by* $\frac{2}{8}$*? What by* $\frac{3}{2}$*?* $\frac{3}{4}$*?* $\frac{3}{8}$*? What by* $\frac{4}{2}$*?* $\frac{4}{4}$*?* $\frac{4}{8}$*? What by* $\frac{6}{2}$*?* $\frac{6}{4}$*?* $\frac{6}{8}$*?* (We might have whole variety, as would be indicated by $\frac{2}{1}$, $\frac{3}{1}$, &c., but it is not used.

I would call attention to the eighth rests at No. 89, and their difference in shape from the quarter rests. After playing 97 I would question about signatures, keys, intervals, &c., as was done at 65. At the lessons in five, six, and seven flats, I should say; it is seen here that some of these lessons are the same in sound as some of those in seven, six, and five sharps, the difference being only in the representation. This difference may be called an enharmonic difference or change. For example, it is said to be an enharmonic change from F sharp to G flat. The teacher may, if he chooses, explain that there is a real difference between these two tones, but that it is so slight as not to be taken into account in tuning pianos, melodeons, &c., nor indeed in any ordinary music. With 98 concludes the learning of the first series of exercises for daily practice; the practice of them should, however, be kept up until the pupil reaches the second series.

### STACCATO.

I would only add to what is printed at No. 100, by saying that I should exercise the pupil a good deal without book, on the Staccato produced by drawing off the fingers. At 103 the last note of each measure in the treble should be accented, and in nearly all the measures the first unaccented. This is another illustration of the fact that the natural accent of the measure is often thrown aside for higher and more tasteful expressions.

### CADENCE. TRANSPOSITION.

At No. 106 I should tell the pupil that any little phrase that will make a good ending either to a section or a piece of music, is called a *Cadence*. I should then play or sing a little melody, perhaps like this:

I would then give it again, beginning on B, (which would make it the key of G,) and would ask if it is the same tune. The answer being given, I would ask if it differs in *any* respect from the first. If the pupil perceives that it does differ in respect to pitch—that it is the same tune, only higher in one case than in the other, I should say that the process of performing the same piece at a different pitch is called *transposition*, and I should try *very hard* to impress him with the idea that to transpose well, is one of the most useful and elegant accomplishments of the musician, and to you, fellow teachers, I would say that if this matter is well followed up from this simple beginning, there is no doubt of its success. It may, however, be best for you to get your pupil to transpose other phrases or short simple melodies beside these, and I would try to have him perceive how pleasant this change is from the key in which he is playing to the one which is a fifth or fourth from it.

At No. 110 the dotted quarter occupies one part and a half, of the measure. It is usually difficult to get right the note which follows this dotted quarter, and which must come in on the last half of one part of the measure. My idea is that it should rather be *felt* than *calculated*, and I have made some preparation in the lesson for this result, as you will see. Some device like counting one and two, and one and two, &c., may sometimes be necesssary, but I should prefer to accomplish the object by getting the right idea of the sound in the mind; and here let me say that

### KEEPING TIME

Is an interior operation. If the pupil thinks too fast, the counts or hand will go too fast. They are, like the hands of a clock, but outward indexes of the controlling power, therefore I should try to have my pupils *feel* the right time, using the hands or counts as regulators, and to aid, perhaps, in keeping the place in the music. By the time the pupil reaches the second series for daily practice, it is probable that he will be ready to give up the first. I should endeavor to interest him in transposing, accenting, and giving the staccato and other expressions to these *exercises*, as they are of great importance. Those commencing at No. 121 are *very valuable* in promoting flexibility of fingers. I should keep up the daily practice of this second series, at least until reaching the fourth series.

### RITARDANDO.

At 126 I should show the pupil the effect called *Ritardando e diminuendo*, (gradually slower and softer,) and point to the abbreviation of the phrases.

*What interval is formed here by the two tones heard together in the treble? What key are you in? What kind of time? Which variety of double time?*

At 127 I should say that RONDO MOVEMENT here signifies that the lesson is in the style that pieces called *Rondos* are usually written in. So it may be said of the lessons marked "Waltz movement," that they mean in the time and character of waltzes, &c.

### THE SCALE.

Before playing No. 128, I should say to the pupil, play the tones of the key of C, from middle C to the next C above. These eight tones make what is called the scale; in this particular case the scale of C. Now commence at G and play the tones of the key of G in the same way. Of course he will now leave out F, as that tone does not belong to the key of G, and will play F♯ instead of it. This is the scale of G. Name the tones that make the scale of C. Name those that make the scale of G. Now the tones of scales, besides having the letteral names that you have just given here, have the names of numbers applied to them in the following order, viz: the key note is always ONE, the next tone TWO, the next THREE, and so on up to eight, and for some purposes they go still higher as nine, ten, &c., but the scale is complete with eight. I should then ask him to tell me what interval is made by one and two of either of these scales. What by two and three, three and four, four and five, five and six, six and seven, and seven and eight; and thus lead him to observe and know the order of the steps and half steps as they are always found in this succession of tones. *Between what tones do half steps occur in the scale? Where are steps found?* In practicing No. 129 be careful of the fingering. It is hardly necessary to repeat that the great work of the teacher all the time is to make the pupil *do* well, for by doing he will not only improve all his musical powers, but will the better *understand*. At the proper time, I would ask such questions as the following:

*What tone is one in the scale of C? What is two? Three? Four? Five? Six? Seven? Eight? What tone is one in the scale of G? What is two? Three? Four? &c.*, (and the same of the other scales.) *Do the half steps occur between three and four and between seven and eight in all these scales? Is it necessary that they should so occur to make the scale sound right? Could this order be so preserved without the tones made by the black keys, and named by flats and sharps?*

It may now be told that the occurrence of the steps and half steps, put in this order, is what makes this series so agreeable, and it is to make these steps and half steps occur in this way, that certain tones are used. Regarding the scale then as a tune, it is here transposed by fifths through all the keys, the same tune having the same intervals in the same order in each case. You will find that successions of tones or runs, sometimes commence and end with other tones than one or eight. For example, in the key of C you may play every tone in succession from G to G, (an octave,) or from D to D, or E to E, &c., but if you play only tones that belong to the key of C, they will be simply different forms of the scale of C.

*What intervals are formed by the left hand part in No. 127?*

At 130 an octave or interval of an eighth occurs in the base. These pieces, with words to them, may be sung as duets, although it is expected that they will usually be performed by one person. Of course an important object of the practice here is to get the wrist motion, and another is an even and smooth running of the scale one octave. Learners sometimes like to strike with one hand before the other, when both should start together. Now is the time to regulate all such things. You perceive that about the same kind of work is to be done in each key.

*As we go from one key and scale to another, by what interval is our transposition?*

It will be well to question with reference to the peculiarities of each piece. Each lesson on page 63 is to be learned in its order. If convenient to have three players, the three numbers will sound well together. At No. 172 another very important series of daily exercises commences. It is probable that the second series may now be given up. I should, however, keep the third with this for the present. On page 68 are three more lessons that may be played together, but each one is important for some particular purpose.

Before playing endeavor to have the pupil avoid the two faults common in appoggiatura playing, viz: striking the appoggiatura *before* the note in the left hand which comes on the same part of the measure, and keeping it down while striking the large note. In No. 185 I should have the pupil play so as to make the melody sound like a song; and in No. 186 make the repeating notes even and distinct. It is good to exercise the imagination in these innocent ways, and I should have him think of sleigh bells in the first, of a song in the second, and the steps of the horses in the third.

## HARMONY. THE COMMON CHORD.

Before playing No. 187 I should say, give me middle C. Now the tone which is a third above it; now that which is a fifth above it, and lastly, that which is an eighth above it. Now combine those tones and give them together with one hand, if the hand is large enough; I would then say, "any tone combined with those that are a third, fifth, and eighth above it, make, when heard together, what is called the common chord. As these tones are reckoned from C, the chord made by them is said to be the common chord of C. Play all the common chords of C that you can find on the piano; that is, take every C in succession for the lower tone of a common chord, (excepting, of course, the upper C.) Which chords sound best, those in the lower, upper, or medium octaves of the instrument? I would then say that the tones of chords are also named with the names of numbers,—that the tone from which you reckon is called one, the next above three, the next five, and the next eight, or one. I would add that in harmony eight and one are often spoken of as the same thing, and that three in one octave is three in the next, &c.—to illustrate, in this common chord of C, every C on the instrument is one or eight, every E three, and every G five. It may now be well to have the pupil understand that the lettoral names describe the abstract or absolute pitch of tones, while the numeral names describe tones as connected or related with each other in families, as scales and chords.

*What is the pitch of one in the common chord of C?* (Ans. C.) *What is the pitch of three? What of five? What of eight?*

Now take G and play with it the tones which are a third, fifth, and eighth above it, and so make the common chord of G. Play every common chord of G. *What is the pitch of one in the common chord of G? What of three? Five? Eight?* We might now make a common chord with F for one, but this is perhaps enough to illustrate the fact that the common chord can be made at any pitch. The pupil by this time may have inferred that any possible combination of the tones C, E, G, C, can make only the common chord of C, but he would not be likely to know that some of these combinations are described by the terms, first position, second position, and third position, and this I would proceed to introduce.

### POSITIONS.

Play the common chord of C with one in the left hand, and three five and eight in the right. When the combination of these tones is such that eight (or one) is the highest, the chord is said to be in its *first* position. Now play it so that E or three will be the highest. This is the *second* position. Now play it so that five will be the highest. This is the *third* position. The lower note or base may be kept one in all these positions. Now play No. 187. If the hand is too small the *one* need not be doubled in the base.

At No. 189 I should endeavor to make clear the important fact, that each tone in these lessons is named in three different ways, and for three different purposes; for example, the first tone in the base has one name for its pitch, another for its place in the key, and another for its place in the chord. It is G as to its pitch; it is five as to its place in the key or scale of C, and it is one as to its place in the common chord of G. (I would draw this from the pupil by questions rather than tell him, if possible.)

### TONIC AND DOMINANT.

At 190 I should say, one in a key or scale is in harmony called the tonic of that key, and five is called the dominant. A chord formed on one is therefore called a *tonic chord*, and a chord formed on five, is called a *dominant chord*. It is, however, very common to say, "Tonic" and "Dominant," when we mean the chord formed on those tones. I think the ear should be not much lifted in playing chords, unless they are to be quite loud. At 194 comes

### SUBDOMINANT.

Four in a key, is called the subdominant, (*under* the dominant,) and the chord on four is the subdominant chord. I should observe the directions printed over the lesson, which would be all that is needful in introducing this chord. At the proper time I should question thus:

*What are the names of the tones that make a common chord? What are the names of the tones that make a scale? What is the pitch of each tone in the scale or key of C?* (Ans. One is C, two D, &c.) *What is the pitch of the tones in the key of C?* (Ans. One is G, two A, &c.) *What is the pitch of one in the common chord of F? What of three? Five? Eight? How many positions have common chords? What is highest in the first position? What in the second? What in the third? How many names has either one of the tones in this lesson, F for example? What are they?* (Ans. F, four, and one.) *What is F the name of as applied to you tone? What is four the name of as applied to it? What is one the name of as applied to it?*

I would ask similar questions of every tone in this key. The pupil will thus be led to notice, for example, that E has *three* for both chord and scale name, and that G has not only *five* for its name in the scale of C and the chord of C, but it is also one in the chord of G, and that C has two chord names, viz: one (in the chord of C,) and *five* (in the chord of F.) *What are the names of D? What of B?* All this will help the pupil to a clearer insight into the subject of music, and to exactness in the use of musical terms.

### VOICE CULTURE FOR SINGING.

While I would not underrate the usefulness and general importance of the study of Physiology, I do not suppose it necessary to know the forms and names of the muscles and other organs of the fingers, hands and arms, in order to play upon the piano or violin, nor of the lips to play upon the trumpet or flute, nor of any other parts of the body in order to walk or dance. As might be inferred, I do not suppose it necessary to know the anatomy of the throat in order to sing, still it is interesting to know something of the way that the voice is produced, and of the organs that have to do with singing, and it is convenient to know some of their names. I therefore append, briefly, some information that I have obtained on this subject; and first,

### THE LUNGS,

Something like sponges, that may be distended or compressed at pleasure, by filling their cells with air and breathing it out again; second,

THE MUSCLES,

Abdominal and intercostal, under and at the sides of the lungs, that do the work of distending and compressing; third,

THE WINDPIPE, OR TRACHEA,

That goes from the lungs to the mouth; fourth,

THE LARYNX,

That holds the most important part of the vocal apparatus; fifth and sixth,

THE PHARYNX AND MOUTH.

Of these important organs referred to in the larynx, (the outer projection of the larynx is called the "Adam's apple;) the first are two muscles which come together something like lips, and which may be opened or shut at pleasure. These muscles are called the "vocal chords," and the opening they make, "the glottis." It is probable that some tones of the voice are produced by forcing the breath between these two lips, when they are near together, and thus making them vibrate, and that other tones are produced by opening these lips wide, and somehow making the air vibrate in the windpipe, on the principle of the flute. If the tone could be heard just as it comes from the glottis, without any mouth or other cavity to resound in, it would probably be anything but agreeable; but fortunately it passes into a small cavity called the pharynx, where it receives its musical quality; then into a larger one called the mouth, where it is perfected, and where it may be formed into words. The pharynx (which may be seen above the roots of the tongue at the top of the throat) being a flexible cavity, may be distended or contracted at pleasure, and the different qualities of tone— as expressive of the different emotions—joy, sorrow, &c., depend wholly upon the right distension or contraction of this organ.

It is not possible to show so definitely here how I would teach singing as playing, because there is so much greater difference in voices than in fingers, nor is it possible to write lessons so exactly suited to all, for the same reason. At No. 199, after seeing that the position of the pupil is right, I should proceed to examine his voice as to quality, compass, and quantity. In doing this I should extend the scale here printed, or make use of other scales, higher or lower, according to his compass.

DELIVERY OF THE VOICE.

I would see first what defect there may be in the giving out or delivery of the voice. For this I would use the syllables, do, re, mi, &c., or "ah," (Mr. Bassini's word "sea," (pronounced seah,) is also excellent,) and would have the pupil sustain each tone with deliberation. The principal obstacles that I have found to giving out or delivering the tone well, are, closing too much the lips and teeth, raising or bulging the tongue in the mouth, and drawing it backward and upward into the throat. I should not now speak of other difficulties that I might discover, on the principle of "one thing at a time."

TAKING BREATH.

I would ask the pupil to take a full breath, by making the muscles, which are at the sides of the lungs, and over the ribs, distend, and at the same time draw in and up the muscles under the lungs, as if he were trying to make himself as small as possible around the waist. When the lungs are thus filled, they seem to press upward, and to be fullest and most distended at the top, which is the best possible position for managing the breath, and for giving the singer confidence that it will not give out. This latter condition is, however, not fully attained, unless the

USE OF THE BREATH

In singing be in the right way, and that includes the two following important things, viz: making use of as little breath as possible, and holding the abdominal muscles firmly in their drawn in position. When the pupil gets well started in this subject of breathing, I should touch upon the subject of

VOWEL SOUNDS.

If practicing with "ah," I should see that it is not "au," or like the vowel sound in the word "learn," but like that of the first syllable in "father." If using the syllables, do, re, mi, I should try to have each one exact and pure in its pronunciation. It is necessary that nearly all the important points about singing should be brought in and understood early, as nothing will sound well if one of them is wrong. Of course the pupil will not get them all right at once, but he will make a beginning, and will have something to work for. So at No. 200 I should begin to speak more definitely of the

FORM OF TONE.

I should say that the Pharynx may be distended so as to make the voice large and hollow, or it may be contracted so as to make it thin, and even sharp; but that in the practice of these exercises, it is best neither to distend nor contract the pharynx, and so not let the tone be either on the one side or the other. If the pupil says that his voice does not seem to mean anything produced in that way, I should tell him that there is nothing here for it to mean; that all we want now is a full, natural, simple utterance of these tones, correct in pitch, and exact in the pronunciation of the syllables applied to them. I should be very careful here, and always, to keep the pupil from striking under the pitch of the tone he is to sing, and then slide it up.

ARPEGGIOS—MELODY MADE OF CHORDS.

Before playing this lesson I should say, play the common chord of C, with the right hand. Now play these tones one after another in any order you please, as This playing the tones of a chord one after another, makes what is called an arpeggio of the chord. Make an arpeggio of the common chord of G. Of F. After going over this lesson two or three times, I would say, the part you play here while singing is called an accompaniment.

What is the first chord in the accompaniment? What tones are sung with it? What are tones of chords called when played or sung after each other instead of all together?

PASSING NOTES.

Before playing No. 201 I would ask the pupil to play the common chord of C, and at the same time sing the tone D—holding the tone and striking the chord three or four times. This he would find unpleasant, because D does not belong to the chord of C. I would then ask him to play and hold the same chord, and move from C to G, about as fast as quarter notes usually go. Now he would find the D and F not unpleasant, although neither belong to the chord he is playing, and so would bring out the fact that you may play or sing pleasantly, tones that do not belong to the chord that accompanies, if you do not dwell too long upon them, and these tones I would name passing notes. Some pupils need to practice with syllables to improve their articulation. This I regard their most important use.

What passing notes occur in the first measure? Are there any in the second? What in the third? &c.

ACCOMPANYING.

At No. 202 I would ask the pupil to strike in one chord the tones of the first and second measures. He would find himself making the common chord of C. I would then ask him to make into a chord the arpeggio in the third measure. He would find this the chord of F. After going through in this way, I would ask him to make an accompaniment to this lesson, by putting into chords with a base, the arpeggios it is composed of.

What chord will accompany the first and second measures here? What the fifth and sixth? &c. Are there any passing notes in this lesson?

I would have the pupil accompany with different positions of the chords. For example, sometimes accompanying the first and second measures with the first position of the chord of C, as in the previous lesson, and sometimes with the second position, and sometimes the third, singing, of course, the same melody. We might tell the pupil here, or even before this, that the part in a piece of music that is the most tuneful, and that the ear catches most readily, is called "the melody."

PHRASING.

To illustrate this subject at No. 203, I would read some sentence without observing the marks of punctuation; stopping for breath where there should be no pause, sometimes even between the syllables of a word. This would be sure to injure, if not destroy the sense and meaning of the sentence.

I would then say that singing through rests, and taking breath or in other ways making stops when there should be none, produces analogous unpleasant results in music. For this reason good management of the breath, and the ability to phrase well, are important things for the musician to acquire. If necessary to a more clear showing of this subject a familiar melody might be taken, and the unpleasant effects of wrong phrases, manifested by the process referred to. In this lesson the phrases are defined by the rests.

*How many tones in the first phrase in this lesson? How many notes? How many phrases in the whole lesson?*

I should give such directions as are printed over these lessons, and should remind the pupil of the importance of observing them when I am away.

### THE CHORD OF THE SEVENTH.

At 204 I should say, play the common chord of G, first position. Now let us make a new chord by playing seven here instead of eight. This is called the chord of the *seventh*.

*What is eight in the chord of G? What then will be seven? The common chord consists of the tones one, three, five, and eight, what does the chord of the seventh consist of?*

Now play it, but let one be the highest instead of seven. Now let three be the highest. Now five. These are the different positions of this chord. As one and eight are treated in harmony as the same, it may be said that the chord of the seventh is made by simply adding seven, to one, three, five, and eight. This is especially true in pianoforte music, where four tones are usually played with the hand giving the chord.

*Are we speaking here of seven of a scale or seven of a chord? What is seven in the scale of C? What is seven in the chord of the seventh of G?*

### QUALITIES OF TONE.

Before practicing No. 206 I would say, all persons who have the capacity to experience the different kinds or grades of joy and sorrow, fear, reverence, awe, &c., have the organs and powers for giving them exact and true expression, and the different sounds of the voice that are used for this purpose are technically called *qualities of tone.* The pharynx is the organ by which the qualities of tone are principally made, and when guided by a right understanding of this subject, and accustomed to be shaped into the right form to express the emotions of the singer, becomes wonderfully sensitive to every shade of feeling. Some singers can so adjust the pharynx to produce one quality of tone, and this they never vary, except to make it louder and softer. If a base, he distends the pharynx perhaps, so that he may get the large or deep quality that he delights in, and this prevails, whatever may be the subject of his song. Such a persons seems always to be thinking of his voice, instead of what he is singing about, and of course never gives a true expression, excepting to words that belong to that quality. Others have preferences for other qualities, and their performances are liable to similar objections, but this one will serve for illustration.

### WORDS FOR SINGING.

I should continue here by saying, that words to be good for singing, must be of a kind to excite emotion; that those which are addressed to the head rather than to the heart, are not fit for music. I would further say that some words are calculated to excite strongly, either the joyful feelings on the bright side, or the sad ones on the dark side, or modifications of them, such as boldness, grandeur, reverence, &c., while others are suited to excite the more quiet emotions—such as are near the line between the bright and the dark. The songs of these "summer scenes," are of this kind, though they all keep on the bright side of the line. I should try to check such tendencies as the pupil might have while singing them, either to distend the pharynx too much, and so produce too *dark* a tone, or to contract it too much, and so err on the other side. It should here be said that when the Pharynx distends, the Larynx should descend, and vice versa. By observing the outer projection of the larynx, while gradually changing from a bright tone to a sombor one, it can be known whether this is so. Distending the pharynx and raising the larynx at the same time, shows the tone to be produced in an injurious manner.

I should endeavor to have the pupil perceive the true correspondence that exists in the nature of things between a certain emotion and the *kind of sound* or quality of tone which is its natural expression. This might be illustrated, if necessary, by calling to his mind the kind of tone that would naturally be made use of in *speaking* under different circumstances; for example, suppose any one deeply impressed and excited by the sublimity of the Falls of Niagara, were to utter some exclamation while gazing upon them, such as "how grand," "how sublime," and you were to analyze, you would find that the *quality* of tone in which those words were uttered, would be exactly correspondent to the emotion that caused them, and the pharynx would be properly distended to produce this result. Let this same person look upon a little brook, rippling and dancing down the hill side, and with real pleasure say, "how pretty," the voice will be thinner, and the pharynx more contracted, for the quality of tone will be exactly correspondent to the emotion which is experienced. How unfortunate that in so much singing this naturalness is thrown off, and words are compelled to be united to qualities of tone that they have no affinity for, while a true and correspondent companions are rent asunder, as, for example, the rich, deep voice, already alluded to, whose quality of tone is always suited to louder or softer expression of the *grand* or somber—let him sing of flowers or the happiness of children, or any of those bright things which give us delight, and while the *words* may say they are bright and beautiful, the tone will say they are ponderous, somber, or dark; or it may be that while the words are suited to *win*, the quality of tone *commands.* You will notice that the quality derived from such a performance is in the voice abstractly, or in the tune, and not in the higher thing, viz: the *subject* of the song. There can be only pain where one hears the words and knows their meaning, and desires to be moved by their true expression, and it is not given. If the pupil says, ought I not to sing always with the pleasantest tone that I can produce, I should say no—the tone that corresponds to, and expresses grief is not so pleasant as the one that expresses joy, and yet it should always be used where grief is to be expressed.

It is proper here to say that examples from the teacher, by singing words with right and wrong qualities of tone, are usually of great use to the pupil. When 'words for music take the form of description in order to excite emotion, the singer should let the imagination bring the scene to his mind, and thus come under its influence as far as he can. It is probably understood that I would not advise any one to come under the influence of words that excite low, coarse, or impure emotions, even though the tune to which they are set may be beautiful and attractive, for that would be something like seeking the companionship of an evil person, because he is dressed in fine clothes.

### REGISTERS.

I will state what seem to be the facts about this subject, and will leave those who make use of this book to reason them according to the voice and needs of the pupil. Most voices, whether male or female, go from their lowest tone, up to the neighborhood of middle C, (say from middle C to the G next above,) with a peculiarly firm and masculine kind of voice, technically called the *lower* or *chest register*, then a rounder and more full kind of voice begins and continues to about one octave above middle C, and this is called in women's voices the *medium register*, and in men's voices the *falsetto.* At about this point another change takes place, and the voice assumes again a firmer and more ringing quality, which continues upward through the remainder of its compass. This is called in women's voices the *upper register*, but in men's voices not named, as it is almost never used. Indeed one can use the second register or falsetto but little, and may low voices not at all, the lower or chest register being that which includes almost all their available tones. Some female voices make excellent use of the few tones of the chest register that are allotted to the sex, while others use it too much and too high, and still others, who from natural organism or neglect, have so little strength in its tones, that they make but little use of it. The medium and upper registers are consequently the most important to the female voice. For such voices as need to pass well from the lower to medium registers, and vice versa the first six exercises are prepared. The directions for their practice are very simple, but the practice itself is often slow in its results.

It is not desirable that the break from one register to the other should be removed, for by it beautiful effects are sometimes produced. The great work is equalizing these registers, and it is accomplished by practicing on the lower tones of the medium register, until they become more firm like those of the lower, and modifying the upper tones of the lower register until they come nearer the quality of the medium. The pupil will find that this can be done by getting right control of the pharynx and other organs of the voice. I should endeavor to keep the pupil, who needs this practice, patiently at it, a little while at a time for some weeks; perhaps months. In this way, only, can habits be formed—habits that will make the doing of things seem to be without volition. Thought and practice make a form or home into which, at the proper time, habit comes to dwell.

### VOWEL AND CONSONANT ELEMENTS.

After practicing awhile on No. 215, I should have the pupil practice also other vowel sounds in the same way, as "au," "oo," the vowel sound in "hat," the one in "learn," and the one in "live." After practicing the consonants, as directed at No. 216, I should add combinations to be given in the same way, such as "md," "rmd," "rmds," "rmdst," "tr," "str," &c., (the r to be a little rolled in the last two.)

### ENUNCIATION. PRONUNCIATION. ARTICULATION.

I would here say that enunciation refers to omitting words, and applies especially to consonants, and that pronunciation refers to the forms of words, and applies especially to vowels; while articulation may be said to be the successive utterance of these elements as they occur in syllables. It will not be necessary to speak of each number here, as the directions over them are explicit, only I should now give more attention to daily exercises—perhaps one-fifth of the time allotted for practicing.

*What is the chord in the first measure of No. 221? Which position? What is the second? Third? &c.* (The introduction of sixteenth notes at No. 222 will now be easily accomplished.) *How many sixteenths are equal to a whole? How many to a half? To a quarter? To an eighth?* (Point out single sixteenths; also groups of two, and groups of four.)

### RESUMÉ.

The instrumental lessons up to No. 187 were to aid the pupil in acquiring the requisite skill and knowledge to commence successfully the study of harmony, and through that to understand more fully the structure of all the music he plays and sings—to have a more interior acquaintance with this art than heretofore.

From No. 187 to this point we have, as it were, laid out the work with which the pupil is to become equally familiar in all the keys. It consists of the following things, viz: Exercises and pieces for the use of the common chord and the chord of the seventh in all their positions. Tonic, dominant and subdominant harmonies, and scales and arpeggios one octave. Also exercises and pieces for forming and delivering the voice, management of the breath, phrasing, enunciation, pronunciation, and quality of tone, together with exercises for accompanying and transposition. In all these things, such Rhythmic, Melodic, and Dynamic combinations occur, as are adapted to the state of the pupil, and all are designed to improve his reading, execution and taste. I should daily impress the pupil's mind with the importance of learning to make his own accompaniments; for this purpose I should take great pains with the exercises designed to accomplish this object. I should try, also, to have him realize that true improvement in music is like growing, slow, and accomplished only by taking proper musical food and exercise, in proper quantities, and at proper times, and by these means adding little by little to this muscle and that muscle of the hand and vocal organs, and to this power and that power both of the intellect and the affections. I will also mention some other things here, that may be applied as occasion offers, and the first is, that the face and general appearance of the singer, as well as the tones he sings, should correspond to the emotion he is expressing. All should be in harmony—not exaggerated, but true and natural. It is a good plan, where it is convenient, to arrange the piano so that the pupil will face those who may be listening to him.

The following direction, which perhaps should have been given before, may be of use when the pupil is inclined to increase his power of voice by a contraction of the throat. After adjusting the vocal organs and mouth as well as you can to produce the tone, simply breathe into the glottis, making at first no effort to produce a loud tone. Increase the power of the tone by stronger breathing, rather than by changing the position of the vocal organs. At every key I would ask questions like the following, as well as those that are printed over the lessons.

*What is tonic in this key? Dominant? Subdominant? What tones make the common chord in the tonic? What the common chord in the dominant? What the same in the subdominant? Where is the chord of the seventh formed? What are the names of its tones in this key? How many names has each tone in this key? What are they?* (Ans. Pitch name, scale name, and chord name.)

I would then ask the names of particular tones, as for example, C in the key of G.

*What is its scale name? What is its chord name in the common chord of C? What is the chord of C? What is the chord of the seventh of D? What is its pitch name?*

The pupil will probably have noticed before this, that there is but one pitch name to each tone, and that it never changes, whatever the key may be, but that the same tone may have many scale and chord names. I sometimes illustrate this by saying I have one name, (G. F. Root) that attaches itself to me under all circumstances, and may be called my absolute name. In my family relations I am called other names, as husband, father, &c. In my musical relations I am called teacher, chorister, &c. In my social relations, friend, neighbor, citizen, &c. Just so each tone has one absolute name, and several relative names.

It is hardly necessary to say that do, re, mi, &c., are no more the names of tones than the words of a piece of poetry are. The names gallopade, quickstep, waltz, &c., I should explain to the pupil as indicating music for different kinds of marching and dancing. To introduce dotted eighth notes at 256 I would play a succession of tones that might be represented by eighths, afterwards prolonging, as it were, the first of each two, and shortening the last, as represented in the eleventh measure.

*How many sixteenths are equal to one-eighth? How many to a dotted eighth?*

At No. 258, and at other places, two melodies are given to one accompaniment. This is to accommodate different kinds of voices. The lungs will increase in capacity by the practice of such exercises as these. At 266 it will be noticed that the left hand sometimes plays two tones of a chord, and the right hand two. This does not change the fact that the position of the chord is decided by whatever is highest. You will notice that in each key there is a lesson for each of the points that we wish the pupil to improve in. He should try hard to have each one perfect, in all respects, so that each one may help him firmly and surely on his way.

At 280 I would play, or have the pupil play, either a chord or melody, first with two tones to a count, and then with three. I would then say that three tones in the time usually given to two in a piece, forms what is called a triplet. The triplet is represented by a group of three notes, with a figure three over or under it.

On page 90 I should expect the pupil to take great interest in finding out and playing the right accompaniments to Nos. 282, 283, and 284. When the pupil has reached page 100, he has learned all the scales, and is ready for the more severe practice of the same, for which he will be prepared by Nos. 314 and 315, which I should have him practice daily, more or less, according to the flexibility or inflexibility of his fingers and thumbs.

At No. 316 transposition again. I have noticed that pupils work at this with great interest, as indeed they do at everything in music, if it is adapted to their state and attainments, and is well presented. If the pupil has done everything well to this point, he will willingly work at this until he can play 316 or 317 without hesitation in any key. The knowledge of the keys that this will give him, will be very useful, and indeed indispensable to a successful prosecution of this Curriculum.

### THOROUGH BASE.

At No. 318, I should simply tell the pupil that he is to fill out the chords, the base and treble being to show, in each case, what chord and what position is to be played. The figure 7 denotes the chord of the seventh; all the rest are common chords. In tunes for voices the highest part is called treble, and the lowest base. The part next above the base is called tenor, and the part just below the treble is called alto.

*In these lessons which of these parts are printed? Which are you to add? Play the first chord in this lesson—what is the treble note? What the alto? What the tenor? What the base?*

I would ask similar questions in other chords of this and other lessons. At the last chord but one in No. 327, the 8 7 indicate quarter notes in the tenor, while the treble, alto, and base are half notes.

At No. 331 I would say, when printing was not so easy, and thorough base more in use, it was the custom for composers of vocal music, especially church music, to give the accompanying organist a base, simply with the figures indicating the chord, written over or under it; this saved him some trouble in copying, and was, perhaps, easier for the organist than playing from all the parts. Playing from all the parts is called *"playing from the score."* Playing *through the base*, or *thorough base*, as it is commonly called, I do not regard as very important, but as it renders the pupil more familiar with chords, and takes but little room, I insert it. In such lessons as No. 332, I would have the pupil answer questions about key, kind of time, chord, passing notes, &c.

I would generally keep about two series of daily exercises going at once, though there must be exceptions to this as a rule, from the fact that certain pupils need more practice in certain things. I rely, greatly upon the hints and directions printed over the lessons, for indicating to you, fellow teacher, many things that I have not room to speak of here.

SUSPENSIONS.

At No. 343 I should introduce this subject by having the pupil play (or by playing myself) suspended chords, similar to those in the lesson. I should do this without book or notes, so that the pupil may learn first of the thing itself.

*What is the first chord in the lesson the suspension of, a common chord or chord of the seventh? Which tone of the chord is suspended, one, three, or five? By what?*

The figuring of this in thorough base would, of course, be 6 5, and the beginning of the next measure 9 8, the beginning of the next 4 3, and so on.

CHROMATIC AND DIATONIC SCALES. ACCIDENTALS.

Before playing 344 I should say, touch every key upon the piano in succession, both white and black, up and down, beginning at middle C. This produces what is called the *chromatic scale.* To represent it we cannot modify the degrees of the staff once for all by flats and sharps in a signature as we do in other scales, but must do so piece by piece, wherever we want one of these degrees to represent a chromatic tone. (You will keep in mind that the *staff* represents the *pitch* of sounds, and that the only use of notes is to tell *what degree* of the staff is to be brought into action, and *how long* it is to be kept in, and therefore that sharps and flats have nothing really to do with notes.) Sharps and flats, when used otherwise than in the signature, are called *accidentals.* Their relative names, under like circumstances are, sharp one, sharp two, &c., and flat seven, flat six, &c. Their pitch names we have already learned. (If the pupil should here ask if some of these tones do not have *two* pitch names, I should say yes, as they are heard on the piano, but strictly speaking C sharp and D flat are not at the same pitch. If an instrument could be tuned perfectly, they would be shown to be different tones.) I would here say that the scale we have heretofore used is called the *Diatonic scale.*

*How many kinds of intervals are there in the chromatic scale? What is it? How many in the diatonic scale? What are they? Where do they occur?*

At No. 347 I should call attention to the fact that the signature makes a certain degree of the staff stand for F♯ instead of F, and that to modify the staff during a piece, so that those degrees shall stand for F again, a new character is used, called a natural. I would here say that the natural is used to change the staff *back again* from the effect of a flat also. This is a good place to state to you, fellow teacher, what I understand to be the rule about the continuance of the effect of an accidental. Its effect continues from where it is written, always through the measure, (unless

contradicted by another accidental,) and beyond, if the last note of the measure is on the degree affected, and the first note of the next measure on the same degree. For example, I should say that the first space here stands for F♯ in the second and third measures.

It would mean no more, no less, if a sharp were placed before every note upon that space.

INVERSIONS OF CHORDS.

Before turning to No. 359, I would say, (after reminding the pupil that one and eight in harmony are regarded as the same thing,)

*How many different tones has the common chord?*

Play the three tones that really make the common chord of C, with one for the lowest or base as usual; now play the same chord, but instead of having one for the lowest or base, as heretofore, let us have three, and let one go up into one of the other parts. Now let five be the base, and let three go up. These are called *inversions* of the chord—when three is the base, the first inversion, and when five is the base, the second inversion. The propriety of the name *inversion*, may be seen in the fact that the lowest becomes highest, and the highest lowest, &c.

So many directions and questions are printed over these lessons, that I need not enlarge here. I would take great interest in the transposition of these cadences. I would ask appropriate questions at each of the lessons on page 111. There is probably no danger, fellow teacher, of your underrating the importance of scales, arpeggios, and other technics, and doubtless you have your own ways of keeping up your pupil's interest in them.

VOCAL EXECUTION.

In practicing the exercises on pages 114 and 115 to "ah," or other vowel sounds for neat execution or articulation of the tones, I should carefully avoid on one side the aspirating of each tone, saying, as it were, ha! ha! ha! &c., and on the other the running of the tones together. They should be like a string of pearls; in a sense distinct, and yet all touching each other. If all the things for which the *first series* (page 74) is for, are now well and firmly started, I should diminish the time of their practice, or in some cases give them up. It is, perhaps, unnecessary to add here to the directions from No. 401 to No. 432. At that point I would introduce

THE CHORD OF THE NINTH,

By saying, play the chord of the seventh of G with seven the highest; now add nine, (A.) This is called the chord of the *ninth*, and is, as it were, made by adding to the chord of the seventh, and is always a dominant chord. (There may be no objection to saying here that there are other kinds of chords of both seventh and ninth that do not occur in the dominant, but that we do not use them for the present.)

I would make no explanation with regard to the change of key here, as the subject is more fully treated on page 122. The pupil cannot fail to derive great advantage from the practice that is directed on page 121, and the work will surely interest him, if the previous steps have been well taken, for he must now be quite familiar with the keys heretofore gone over. More time should now be given to technics, if the pupil begins to realize their usefulness, and to like them.

MODULATION.

Before playing No. 442 I should say, play the *direct* common chord of the tonic in the key of C, either position. Now play the direct common chord of the dominant, choosing a position that will cause as little movement of the upper part as possible in going from one chord to the other. I would have these two chords played alternately until the pupil feels fully that he is in the key of C, and then would say, while playing the chord of G, (which is now dominant) you may make up your mind to consider it a tonic chord, and as such may follow it with the chord of D, which is the dominant in the key of G, and so pass from the key of C pleasantly to the key of G.

After playing tonic and dominant until you feel that you are in the key of G, should you wish to return to the key of C, you may do so by making the chord of G (now tonic) a dominant chord. If you wish to make *sure* that it is a dominant chord, I should advise you to put a seventh in it, as our chord of the seventh is always a dominant chord. This kind of going from one key to another is called *modulation*. The tone in the key of G that does not belong to the key of C is, of course, the means by which the modulation is made to the key of G, and the tone which belongs to the key of C, and not to the key of G, is the means by which you go pleasantly back again, and both are called *tones of modulation.*

*What is the tone of modulation in going from the key of C to the key of G? To what chord does it belong in this lesson? What is the tone of modulation in going back to C?*

In No. 444 it will be seen that a modulation takes place to the key of F by means of the tone B flat. It will also be seen that some accidentals occur which do not cause modulation or change of key, but are merely passing notes. If the teacher chooses to introduce these new things, according to the *finding out* plan, so much the better, but I have not room to enlarge in every case.

### SOLFEGGIOS.

But little need be added to what is said on page 124. I should endeavor to have the pupil so control the pharynx, and other organs that give the form for *quality of tone*, that the emotion to be expressed may be evident and consistent throughout. I should give this *solfeggio* at least three expressions, viz: plaintive, (by some distension of the pharynx,) gay, (by some contraction,) and commanding, (by some distension, with more power and intensity or solidity of tone, and decision in enunciation.) It will be important to observe that an effective vocal performance depends not only upon a correct observance of the usual rhythmic, melodic, or dynamic rules and right quality of tone, but very much upon distinct and neat enunciation, pure pronunciation, and an appearance and manner in every way accordant with the emotion to be expressed.

### MINOR SCALES AND CHORDS.

Before No. 451, I should say, strike the A that is next below middle C. Now give me a succession of eight tones, (a scale,) beginning with this A, but use such tones as will produce successively the intervals that I now call for. Step, half step, step, step, half step, step and a half, half step. (A, B, C, D, E, F, G♯, A.) This order of intervals produces what is called the *minor scale.* This particular one is called the scale of *A minor.* The scale we first had is called the *major scale.*

### MAJOR AND MINOR THIRDS.

You remember that it was said early in the course, that there are different kinds of seconds, thirds, fourths, &c. We have now occasion to notice the different kinds of thirds. Play middle C and the E next above it together. This produces a third. Now play the same C with E flat. This also produces a third, but very different in effect.

*Of how many steps is the first third composed? The second?*

A third, consisting of two steps, is called a *major third.* A third, consisting of a step and a half step, is called a *minor third.* Play middle C with the A next below it.

*What kind of a third is here produced?* (Play C♯ with the same A.) *What kind of a third is this?*

Now let us make some common chords, taking the tones from this scale of A minor; and first make a common chord with A for one. You know the common chord consists of a tone, its third, fifth, and eighth. If the third is minor, it is called a *minor common chord;* if the third is major, it is called a *major common chord. Which is this?* It is believed that what is printed in addition on page 128 is sufficient for the beginning of this subject.

### HARMONIC AND MELODIC MINOR SCALES.

I will just state here the facts about the two minor scales at No. 455, leaving you to infer how I would introduce the new one. There are several kinds of minor scales, of which, however, these two are mostly used. The one ascending and descending differently is called the *melodic minor scale,* and the other (the one we have introduced), the *harmonic minor scale.* I should have the pupil examine the intervals of the melodic, and I should ask him such questions as would help him to a clear understanding of both.

Perhaps it may here be seen that the reason why G♯ is not made a signature of the key of A minor, is that G is a tone that belongs regularly to one of the minor scales, and consequently has as much right to be in the signature as G♯, using the term signature in its broadest sense, viz: such an adjustment of the staff as makes it stand for a certain key.

### RELATIVE KEYS.

It may as well be said here that each signature in music is the sign of two keys; a major key and a minor key, and that these are said to be related to each other. For example, the key of A minor is said to be the relative minor of the key of C major, and vice versa, both having the same signature, (natural.) The key of G major and the key of E minor, are similarly related, both having for signature one sharp, &c. I am led here by the remark of a friend to say a few words about

### TECHNICAL TERMS.

For naming different things and operations in sciences, arts, and occupations, words are often taken from their ordinary uses, and a specific or technical meaning given to them. For example, the little iron or brass instrument into which the printer first puts the type as he prepares this work for publication, is called a *stick*, and the operation of setting the type is called *composition.* It would be absurd to say that these words are not appropriate, because their usual meanings are so different. When we say that one key in music is no more natural than another, we use the word natural, according to its common signification; but when we say that the signature to the key of C major is *natural;* or when we speak of the with the *naturalness* of the one nor the other, we have nothing whatever to do with the *naturalness* of the one nor the other, but refer wholly to the technical meaning of the words, just as printers when using the words *stick* and *composition* have no thought of a piece of wood, nor of the literary or musical work which is called composition. Though you cannot take a *half step* when you are walking, nor give a *half tone* when you are singing, you do not thereby hinder, in the least, the use of those words as technical terms. Some of the words used as technical terms have meanings that are very similar in their different uses, and so seem quite appropriate, while in others there seems to be no similarity nor appropriateness, and we should perhaps wonder why they were chosen, if it was a matter of much importance.

### TONIC DOMINANT AND SUBDOMINANT IN THE MINOR.

Each minor key has its own scales, chords and harmonics, on the same general plan as the major, though producing very different musical effects; and at the proper time I should make sure by questioning, and other means, that the pupil understands these relations as well in the minor as in the major. By the time the pupil has reached page 150, if he has done his work well, he will have become well grounded in the things which this time going through is intended to teach, and besides, will have improved in reading, execution, and taste. By this time your plan, fellow teacher, is probably fixed. If it is thorough; if no lesson is left until it is so well learned that the pupil can play it easily, surely, and gracefully, under any circumstances, if the singing, especially that which relates to qualities of tone, is well understood and practiced, if reasons for all things are so clear that everything is viewed in rational light, if reviews are well made, and the whole work well balanced, then I am sure the pleasant picture drawn a few pages back, is, in your case realized.

After preparing the pupil to practice No. 513, I would try to have him understand, for example, that the three first chords in this lesson are, in harmony but different forms of the same chord, one being the same tone in each, and that we play the chord of whatever is one, consequently not always the chord of the *written base,* that being sometimes three, sometimes five, and sometimes seven. I would also have him understand that in order to know what chord to play, we must know where one is, and that this is found out by the figure or figures; the base being three when the figure 6 is under it, five when ⁶₄, &c. A few questions adapted to the state of the pupil, in addition to what is printed with the lessons, especially after they have been played a few times, will render everything about this not very intricate matter, sufficiently clear. I will only add about the lessons on page 152 that they are designed especially for improvement in flexibility of voice, and that the tones should not be made too separate, nor too much run together, but may always be sung as fast as they can be neatly articulated. No. 534,

SHOCK OF THE GLOTTIS.

While it is easy to *show* how I would do this, it is difficult to describe it, so as to be sure of being understood. To repeat a tone while singing only a vowel sound, requires a sudden shutting and opening of the glottis, called the *shock of the glottis*. It is as though the breath, being dammed up, suddenly burst out. Care should be taken that the muscles which control the breathing act suddenly, and that the breath does not press too hard against the glottis. I should pass on through all these technics trying to infuse in to my pupil's mind an appreciation of their usefulness, and a love for their practice, which, however, can only be done by his perceiving the benefit they are to him, and this result is, of course, only reached by practicing them daily and faithfully, until the inflexible or stubborn muscles and chords yield to their influence.

DOUBLE DOTTED NOTES.

At No. 553 I would say, give me a tone three beats or counts long. *What kind of note will represent this?*

Now give me a tone a half beat longer than that, or as long as a half note, quarter note, and eighth note. This may be represented by a double dotted half note. It may be said that the second dot always adds to the note as much as half the value of the first dot.

*A double dotted quarter note will be equal in length to what notes?* To *what counts here?* *How many parts of the measure will it fill?*

*Calculation* will, perhaps, help here at the beginning, but a certain appreciation or feeling with regard to this rhythmic form should be the governing power.

ETUDE.

I have no desire to use foreign words when those of our own language will answer just as well, but "study" no more gives the full significance of *étude* than "rather slow" does of "andante." Étude, though a French word, has come into general use, as the name of a certain kind of music that often embodies the beauties of the choicest pieces, but always has reference to the improvement of the player in some particular direction. Études are much used for concert and parlor playing. I should say to the pupil it is pleasant and useful, while practicing these pieces to make them, in your imagination, descriptive of their titles. With the solfeggios beginning on page 157, I should leave the pupil more to his own resources in phrasing, making use of vowel sounds or syllables, as might be most useful to him. The expedient to save room on pages 158 and 159 will not, I hope, prevent the use of these excellent exercises which are taken from a new book by Wolfahrt, as are those also on page 164. With regard to the Études in which relative keys are used, I would ask at various points,

*How many keys in each signature the sign of?* *What are they called?* *What is the major key here?* *What the minor?* *What is relative major to —— minor?* *What is relative minor to —— major?*

I should call attention to the beautiful effects of minor music, and try to have my pupil like them. No one can play the scales, accenting in each kind of time, according to the models on page 168, without being greatly improved, both in execution and a knowledge of the keys. Need I say a word here, fellow teacher, about the paramount *importance* of having our pupils now know all the scales and their fingering by HEART? I certainly should, as soon as possible, hear all scale practice *without the book*. Although these models occupy but little room here, they will, if rightly practiced, occupy an important place in the time and interest of the pupil for many weeks. This is the case in this book, with many lessons that look simple, and occupy but little space.

CADENZA.

It happens sometimes, both in playing and singing, that the rhythmic equality of a piece of music is broken into by a flight of tones, (generally either just before a closing cadence, or between sections,) that serves either as a graceful flourish or a connecting chain, and is subject to no other rhythmic law than the taste of the performer, not being usually marked into measures. This is called a *cadenza*, and is usually written in smaller

notes. The piece seems to stop, while the cadenza steps in and gives its performance, and then resumes its movement. An appropriate cadenza, well performed, gives much pleasure to musicians.

THE GRAND PRACTICE OF THE SCALES.

At page 176 I should much have liked to print all the scales here to be practiced, but it would have taken *twenty-four* pages, and would, at the same time, have deprived the pupil of the great advantage of exercising his own powers in transposition, neither of which, fellow teacher, could we afford. I well know, that even with all the scales and their fingering by heart, our pupils here have a great work to do; one that will occupy a part of each day for months—certainly many weeks. Especially will this be the case if each model is accented in the four ways given on page 168, and so practiced in every key.

THE IMPERFECT COMMON CHORD.

Before playing No. 670 I would say, play a fifth, with middle C for the lowest tone.

*Of how many steps and half steps is this interval composed?* From C to G there is a fifth made of three steps and a half step. This is called a *perfect fifth.* Now play G flat for the upper tone.

A fifth composed of two steps and two half steps is called an *imperfect fifth.* Now play the common chord of C major. Now play E flat instead of E, and so produce the minor common chord of C. Now the same with G flat instead of G, and you will have the *imperfect common chord* of C. I would then aid the pupil to investigate and find out that the major common chord consists of a major third, perfect fifth, and octave; that the minor common chord consists of a minor third, perfect fifth, and octave; and that the imperfect common chord consists of a minor third, imperfect fifth, and octave. He would see that the minor common chord is named from the third, and the imperfect common chord from the fifth.

*How many kinds of common chords are there?* *What are they called?* *Of what are they composed?* &c.

It would be an excellent plan to have the pupil form the three kinds of common chords successively on each tone of the scale, thus:

SUPERTONIC. MEDIANT. SUBMEDIANT. LEADING NOTE.

I should say that as one in any key is called the tonic, so two is called the *supertonic,* (above the tonic,) three the *mediant,* (midway between tonic and dominant,) six the *submediant,* (midway between submediant and tonic,) and seven the *subtonic,* (under the tonic.) This last is, however, mostly known by its harmony name of *leading-note.* As chords are formed on tonic, dominant, and subdominant, so they may be formed on these other tones. The pupil will soon perceive that of these new chords, or rather on these new places for chords, only one imperfect common chord is formed, the others being minor. Preparing for 671 is only playing one, three, five, and seven, on each tone of the scale successively, thus:

While the pupil does this, I would ask what intervals these chords are composed of, but first would show that there are two kinds of interval of the seventh; a major seventh, consisting of five steps and one half step, and a minor seventh, consisting of four steps and two half steps. In this first chord he will see there is a major third, a perfect fifth, and a major seventh.

*What kind of a seventh is used in the chord of the dominant seventh that we have been practicing?*

I should prepare for the practice of 672 and 673 by saying that music is mostly made of tonic, dominant and subdominant harmonies, they being used in every conceivable form of position and inversion, and that these new chords are limited in their use, hardly ever appearing in more than two or three forms. I should have the pupil play these cadences in all the keys, and answer such questions about the use of the new chords as will help him them in his mind. I should present some things for investigation in the way so often spoken of, that I don't mention here for want of room. For example, the fact stated at No. 672, about certain chords of major keys, having different names in the relative minor. It may be stated at 674 that

3

there are still other resolutions of the chord of the seventh than those of the tonic and subdominant, but they will be easily understood.

*What is tonic in the key of A minor? What is submediant in the key of C major? What is subdominant in the key of A minor? What is supertonic in C major?*

I would ask similar questions of chords in other relative major and minor keys. I would also ask the pupil to tell me all the names of a chord as it occurs in different keys, as for example, that the chord of A minor is tonic in the key of A minor, submediant in C major, supertonic in G major, subdominant in E minor, &c.

THE CHORD OF THE DIMINISHED SEVENTH.

At No. 675, I would say that there is still another kind of interval of the seventh, which is formed by taking a minor seventh, and substituting for the *lower* tone, one which is a half step higher, and that this new interval is called the *diminished* seventh. I might illustrate thus: The directions are so full with this lesson, that it is not necessary to say more here.

THE CHORD OF THE EXTENDED SIXTH.

Before practicing No. 676, I should show the three kinds of intervals of the sixth, and find out about them in the way already mentioned, and then say that this chord is named from the larger of these three sixths. It may easily be seen that this chord is really a chord of the seventh, and would be figured ⁴₃, but with sharps or naturals before the G and J, according to the key in which it is used. The naming of chords by the thorough base figuring has already been spoken of, and by such naming this would be "The chord of the extended sixth, the sharp fourth and the third." It may be interesting here to observe that the major common chord is named from the fact that it has a major third, the minor common chord from the minor third, the imperfect common chord from the imperfect fifth, the chord of the seventh from the seventh, &c.

At No. 678, and at all the songs, I should have the pupil analyze the harmony, naming the chords with their modulations and passing notes, exercising especial care in regard to the *quality* of the tone.

At No. 679, it would only be necessary to show that a tone is also syncopated when it commences on the last half of a beat, and continues through the first half of the next beat. This rhythmic form should, when learned, be *felt*, rather than calculated. Putting the syncopated part of No. 680 into eighth notes at first, may be useful, thus: &c.

EMBELLISHMENTS.

It is only necessary to add to what is said at Nos. 682 and 700, that all ornaments or embellishments depend for their success not only upon being well chosen and neatly executed, but upon a certain good judgment and taste in making them faster or slower, according to circumstances. There can be no substitute for the living example in acquiring these and many other things in music. Pupils cannot *guess* at good style; they must hear it both from us and good public performers, as opportunity may offer.

PEDAL HARMONY.

At No. 683, I would play the first four measures of the lesson, *keeping* the base C, and would say that this keeping the same base while the rest of the harmony changes, produces what is called *Pedal Harmony*. Although pedal harmony may be very easy to do, considerable attainment in the appreciation of music is required before it is really liked.

At No. 686 the three chords of the diminished seventh are given, the first position of each in full, the others are left to be finished by the pupil, which I should have thoroughly done, choosing the fingering with great care.

With regard to the three kinds of études here made use of, I would say that the études progressives, have for their principal object improvement in various things of execution, the études élégantes, though still designed to help the pupil in execution, have especial reference to taste, while the études caractéristiques endeavor to embody both the former things in some of the more unusual and characteristic styles of music.

PEDALS.

At No. 703, I should say that the pedal which lifts the dampers from the strings should be used rather to prolong tones than to make them louder. The term *loud pedal* is an unfortunate one, as it leads to wrong ideas of its use. The foot should be pressed upon the pedal at the word "ped," and lifted at the star. The effect of this will be to continue the tone sometime after the fingers have left the keys, and thus make the chords fuller, and the harmony richer.

Holding the pedal down for the purpose of making the instrument loud, especially if by so doing, chords or tones are run together that should be distinct, is a bad habit, injurious to the perceptions and taste of the player, and disagreeable to persons of musical culture. Such a course is sometimes resorted to in the hope of concealing defects in execution.

In the scales in thirds and sixths I should have the pupil play a part of the time legato. To do this it is important that one finger or thumb at least should remain on the keys until the next third or sixth is struck. Each of the remaining pieces and songs should in turn be analyzed and understood as to their construction, and as far as possible the intention of the author with regard to their performance should be carried out. The first of these things will be easily done by going over the pieces slowly, having the pupil name the different things of their harmony. The other is more difficult, and consists not only in observing and doing all the external things, such as giving each note its exact value, taking the right movement, executing with grace and neatness, using the pedal skillfully, giving the cres. and dim., and all other dynamic expressions well, but in having him enter, as it were, into the feeling of the composer, and give forth the true musical thought from his (the pupil's) own affection.

In conclusion let me say to you fellow-teacher that an instruction book is properly preparatory, and should be, as it were, a gate which admits the pupil to the extensive and beautiful fields wherein are found the choice flowers and gems of the greater masters. The book that tries to be both the gate and the field must fail in both, as the principle of true progression does not admit of reaching the latter within the limits which every instruction book must have. When the pupil has finished this book rightly, he will not be in the field, but the gate will be open, and he will have already gathered some of the little flowers at its threshold.

GEO. F. ROOT.

DIAGRAM. COMPASS OF SEVEN OCTAVE PIANO.

# GLOSSARY.

ABBREVIATION, besides its usual meaning as applied to musical terms, it is the name of a character that indicates the repetition of the previous group or measure. It is made thus: ⸫, or simply of short lines ≈ corresponding to the dashes on the notes of the group to be repeated.

ACCELERANDO or ACCEL. gradually faster.

ACCENT, more force on the tones of certain parts of the measure. *Natural accent*, in double and triple measure, more force on the first part; in quadruple measure, on the first and third parts; in sextuple measure, on the first and fourth parts. *Accent of Syncopation*, more force where the syncopated tone commences. *Accent of the legato mark*, when the legato mark includes but two or three short notes, more force on the first, whatever may be the part of the measure on which it occurs. Accents are indicated at the pleasure of the composer by these signs ≈ placed over or under notes. Strong and sudden accents are indicated by FORZANDO and its abbreviations.

ACCIDENTAL, a sharp, flat, or natural, used elsewhere than in the signature.

ADAGIO, a very slow movement.

AD LIBITUM, or AD LIB., or A PIACERE, at pleasure—usually indicating a slower movement.

AFFETTUOSO, or AFFET. with tenderness and pathos.

AGITATO, in an agitated manner.

AIR, a term often applied to the principal melody in a composition.

AL, to the; as *al segno*, to the sign.

ALLA, in the style of, as *alla capella*, in the church style.

ALLEGRETTO, somewhat cheerful but not so quick as allegro.

ALLEGRO, quick, lively.

AMOROSO, or CON AMORE, affectionately, tenderly.

ANDANTE, a rather slow movement usually in a gentle and flowing style.

ANDANTINO, a little faster than andante but in similar style.

ANIMATO, animated.

APPOGGIATURA, a small note which not being provided with a regular place in the measure as other notes are, indicates a tone that takes the time of its performance from one of its neighbors.

ARPEGGIO, the tones of a chord performed one after another.

ASSAI, very; as *allegro assai*, very quick.

A TEMPO, in time, used after a change in the movement, to indicate the original time.

AUGMENTED FIFTH, a fifth consisting of four steps.

AUGMENTED SECOND, a second consisting of a step and a half.

AUGMENTED SIXTH, a sixth consisting of five steps.

AUTHENTIC CADENCE. See CADENCE.

BARS, vertical lines across the staff used to divide it into the little portions which are the signs of measures, and which are, for brevity, usually called measures. A bar is sometimes also placed in vocal music at the end of each line of the poetry, and a double bar is always used at the close of a piece of music, and sometimes at the close of a section.

BARITONE, a male voice which as to its compass is intermediate between base and tenor.

BEN, well; as *ben marcato*, well marked.

BIS, a word which written over a phrase indicates that it is to be performed twice.

BRACE, a character used to connect the staves upon which the different parts of the same tune are represented.

CADENCE, the last two or three tones or chords of a section or piece of music. *Half cadence*, the ending of a section on the dominant, *Plagal cadence*, a cadence in which the last chord but one is subdominant. *Authentic cadence*, in which the last chord but one is dominant.

CADENZA, a phrase or strain of music usually rapid and florid, introduced at certain places in certain kinds of music. The rhythmic movement of the piece usually stops for its performance and it is generally represented without bars and in small notes.

CANTABILE, a term describing or indicating a singing and graceful style.

CHORD, three or more different tones given together.

CHORD OF THE NINTH, a tone and its third, fifth, seventh and ninth. The chord of the dominant ninth has a major third, perfect fifth, minor seventh and major ninth. All other chords of the ninth are produced by different inversions or positions of those here named.

CHORD OF THE SEVENTH, a tone and its third, fifth and seventh. The chord of the dominant seventh has a major third, perfect fifth and minor seventh. The chord of the diminished seventh has a minor third, imperfect fifth and diminished seventh. Another chord of the seventh considerably used, has a minor third, perfect fifth and minor seventh.

CHROMATIC SCALE, See SCALE.

CLEFS, characters used to make the staff indicate the absolute pitch of tones. These two [symbol] [symbol] called respectively the treble clef and the base clef, are most commonly used. It may be said of clefs that their use has reference to the employment of as few added degrees as possible. It should also be said that when the treble clef is used in vocal music for the part called tenor, it makes the staff indicate a pitch an octave lower than when used in any other way.

CODA, a second or added ending.

COMMODO, composedly, quietly.

COMMON CHORD, a tone and its third and fifth. The major common chord has a major third and perfect fifth, the minor common chord has a minor third and perfect fifth, and the imperfect common chord has a minor third and imperfect fifth.

CON, with, as *con fuoco*, with fire.

DA CAPO, from the beginning, literally, from head.

D.C., from the ; as *Dal Segno* from the sign.

DIATONIC, a term describing any succession or combination of tones in any key in which no chromatic tones are found.

DIMINISHED FOURTH, a fourth consisting of one step and two half steps.

DIMINISHED SEVENTH, a seventh consisting of three steps and three half steps.

DIMINISHED THIRD, a third consisting of two half steps.

DISSONANT, a name applied to either of the chords of the seventh and ninth, and by some to the second inversion of the common chord; also to certain intervals.

DOLCE, DOL., or DOLCEMENTE, sweetly.

DOLENTE, or CON DOLORE, sadly, sorrowfully.

DOMINANT, the name in harmony sometimes given to a fifth of a diatonic scale.

DOT, see definition of note.

DYNAMICS, the name of the department in music that treats of the power of sounds. The following are the names and signs of the principal things included in it : Pianissimo (*pp*) very soft; piano (*p*) soft; mezzo, (*m*) medium ; forte (*f*) loud ; fortissimo (*ff*) very loud; crescendo (*cres.* or ═══◁) increase; diminuendo (*dim.* or ▷═══) diminish; ◁═══▷ swell; forzando (*fz.* or ▷) a sudden, short, loud tone.

ESPRESSIVO, or } with expression.
CON ESPRESSIONE, }

E, and, as *dim. e ritard*, diminish and retard.

EIGHTH, the interval made by a tone and the next but six to it in the order of a diatonic scale.

ETUDE, the name of a certain kind of composition. See page 17.

FALSETTO, the name given to the middle register of mens' voices. See page 13.

FIFTH, the interval made by a tone and the next but three to it in the order of a diatonic scale.

FINE, end, finis.

FLAT, the name of a character (♭) that is used to make a line or space of the staff, indicate a pitch a half step lower than it would if there were no character but the clef upon it. When the flat is used as a' signature its power is more extended than when used as an accidental.

FORZANDO, (fz,) in piano music a strong accent; in singing a strong accent on the first part of a tone followed by a sudden diminuendo to a less degree of force.

FOURTH, the interval made by a tone and the next but two to it in the order of a diatonic scale.

FUNDAMENTAL BASE, the place that one of a chord would occupy were it in the base.

FUOCO, see con.

GAIO, GAI, gaimento, gaily.

GALOP, the name given to a lively kind of music usually in double measure.

GIUSTO, justly, in exact time.

GRAZIOSO, con Grazia, gracefully.

HALF STEP, a name sometimes given to the smallest interval used in music.

HARMONY, two or more parts performed together. The name given to the whole subject of chords and their progressions.

IL, the; as Il tento, the melody.

IMPERFECT FIFTH, a fifth consisting of two steps and two half steps.

INTERLUDE, a short section usually between repetitions of the main composition.

INTERVAL, the difference of pitch between two tones. The smallest interval in common use is called a half step, and also for certain purposes a minor second. The next larger interval is called a step, and sometimes a major second. This interval may be so represented that its proper name will be a diminished third. The next larger interval is called a minor third, or augmented second. The next a major third or diminished fourth, &c. The names steps and half steps are used to describe the intervals of scales and of other intervals.

INVERSION, a term applied to a chord when the base is any other note than one.

KEY, the term applied to a family of tones bearing a certain relation to each other as to pitch. Seven tones are required to make a complete key, although it may be manifested with fewer. The key of C major consists of the tones A, B, C, D, E, F, G. The key of G major, A, B, C, D, E, F sharp, G. The key of F major, A, B flat, C, D, E, F, G. The key of A minor, (Harmonic) A, B, C, D, E, F, G sharp, A. (In the key of A minor, melodic, both F and F sharp are used.) The family or relative names of the tones of a key are, like those of scales, the same as the names of numbers.

KEY NOTE, That tone of a key which makes the most satisfactory ending or resting place. It is always one in the key, whether the tones of the key are given in the form of a scale, an exercise or a tune.

LARGO, a very slow movement implying a certain seriousness or solemnity.

LEADING NOTE, The name sometimes given to seven of a diatonic scale.

LEGATO, linked together; connected. Legato mark ⌢ a character that stands for legato.

LEGGIERO, LEGGIEREMENTE, lightly.

L'ISTESSO TEMPO, in the time of the previous movement.

LENTANDO, slower and slower.

LENTO, slow.

L. H., left hand.

LOCO, a term used after signs which make the staff indicate a pitch an octave higher or lower than usual, to show that its previous signification is to be resumed.

MA, but; as allegro ma non troppo, quick but not too much so.

MAESTOSO, with majesty.

MAIN DROITE, M. D., right hand; Main Gauche, M. G., left hand. M. S. also stands for left hand.

MAJOR, a term applied to any key, scale, or common chord in which one and three produce a major third; also applied to certain intervals.

MAJOR NINTH, a ninth consisting of six steps and two half steps.

MAJOR SCALE, see scale.

MAJOR SEVENTH, a seventh consisting of five steps and a half step.

MAJOR SIXTH, a sixth consisting of four steps and a half step.

MAJOR SECOND, a second consisting of a step.

MAJOR THIRD, a third consisting of two steps.

MARCATO, detached, but not so much so as staccato; also the name of the dot which indicates this style.

MEASURE, a portion of time. Each measure is divided into smaller equal portions called parts of measures. Measures are represented to the eye by those parts of the staff which are found between bars. Parts of measure are not indicated in written music but are manifested by beats or counts. There are four kinds of measures in common use, viz.: double measure, consisting of two parts; triple measure, consisting of three parts; quadruple measure, of four parts; and sextuple measure, of six parts. In the performance of music a tone may occupy in duration one part of a measure, another tone may occupy two parts, another three or more, another tone may occupy a half or quarter of one part, another a part and a half, &c. Kind and variety of measure are indicated by figures at the commencement of a piece of music, as ⁴⁄₄ quadruple measure quarter variety—quarter variety meaning the value of a quarter note to each part.

MEDIANT, the name in harmony sometimes given to three of a diatonic scale.

MEDLEY, several airs (usually well known) performed immediately after each other.

MELODICS, the name of the department in music that treats of the pitch of sounds. The following are the names of the principal things that belong to it: The major, minor, and chromatic scales, the staff, intervals, degrees, (lines and spaces of the staff,) clefs, A, B, C, &c., (the names of absolute pitch,) one, two, three, &c., (the names of relative pitch,) do, re, mi, &c., (syllables sometimes used in vocal music for purposes of enunciation and pronunciation, or to aid in getting the right pitch,) base, alto, tenor, treble, sharp, flat, natural, transposition, key, trill, turn, and other embellishments, chords, modulations, and other things of harmony.

MELODY, most commonly used to describe that one of several parts in a piece of music which has the most tune, and which is most readily caught and remembered; generally the highest part in a composition for several voices. It also means a succession of single tones differing in pitch.

METRONOME, see page 5.

MEZZO SOPRANO, a female voice whose compass is between that of the soprano and alto.

MINOR, a term applied to any key, scale or common chord in which one and three produce a minor third; also applied to certain intervals.

MINOR NINTH, a ninth consisting of five steps and three half steps.

MINOR SCALE, see scale.

MINOR SECOND, a second consisting of a half step.

MINOR SEVENTH, a seventh consisting of four steps and two half steps.

MINOR SIXTH, a sixth consisting of three steps and two half steps.

MINOR THIRD, a third consisting of a step and a half step.

MODERATO, moderately.

MOLTO, literally much, but usually translated very, as molto allegro, very quick.

MORDENTE, the name of an embellishment, and of the sign ⁓ which indicates it. See page 18.

MOSSO, movement; as piu mosso, more movement, or quicker.

MOTO, anxiety; con moto, with anxiety or agitation.

NATURAL, a character (♮) properly used only where the signification of a line or space of the staff needs to be changed from the effect of a flat, sharp, double flat or double sharp, to the meaning it had before either of those characters were placed upon it.

NINTH, the interval made by a tone and the next but seven to it in the order of a diatonic scale.

NOCTURNE, a certain kind of musical composition. See page 207.

NON, not; see definition of Ma.

NOTATION, a general name for all the signs and terms in the representation of music, that address the eye.

NOTE, a character used to represent the length or duration of a tone. A note, although usually representing the same length throughout the same tune, is made to represent different lengths in different tunes, and therefore cannot be said to have an absolute signification in this respect. The following are the different kinds of notes in common use, with their names : ♩ quarter note, very commonly representing the length of one part of a measure ; ♫ half note, representing (in the same tune) a length equal to that represented by two quarter notes ; ♫· dotted half note equal to that represented by three quarters ; ○ whole note, equal to four quarters ; ○· dotted whole note, equal to six quarters ; ○·· double dotted whole note, equal to seven quarters ; ♪ eighth note, indicating a length equal to half that of a quarter note; ♪· dotted quarter note, equal to three eighths ; ♪·· double dotted half note, equal to seven eighths ; ♬ sixteenth note, equal to half an eighth ; ♬· dotted eighth, equal to three sixteenths ; ♬·· double dotted quarter, equal to seven sixteenths ; ♬ thirty second note, equal to half a sixteenth ; ♬· dotted sixteenth, equal to three thirty-seconds ; ♪ double dotted eighth, equal to seven thirty-seconds. When eighths, sixteenths, or thirty-seconds, dotted or otherwise, are grouped together, they assume various forms, of which the following are the most common :

It may be said of notes that they show which degrees of the staff shall, as it were, be brought into successive or simultaneous action, and that thus they indicate the order or succession of tones.

A group of three notes with the figure three over or under it, thus,

indicates a length equal to that which would be indicated by two of the same kind of notes under other circumstances.

OBLIGATO, a term often applied to one of the intermediate or lower parts in vocal music, when it is designed to have for the time unusual prominence and importance. It is also applied to a part or instrument in the orchestra under similar circumstances, as trumpet obligato, song with violoncello obligato, &c.

OCTAVE, an eighth.

OTTAVA, or 8va, octave. This term makes that part of the staff over which it is placed indicate a pitch an octave higher. It also makes that part of the staff under which it is placed indicate a pitch an octave lower.

PASSING NOTES, names given to some of the tones (generally short) that do not form part of the chords with which they are played or sung, and also to the notes that represent them. See page 12.

PAUSE, ⌒ a character which indicates that the value of a note or rest over which it is placed is to be increased, usually about twice its length. When placed over a double bar it indicates the close of a piece of music.

PED., pedal.

PERFECT FIFTH, a fifth consisting of three steps and a half step.

PERFECT FOURTH, a fourth consisting of two steps and a half step.

PHRASE, the smallest division of a piece of music that contains, so to speak, a musical idea.

PIACERE, see ad lib.

PITCH, one of the three essential properties of a tone; its highness or lowness.

PIU, more.

POCO, a little; as poco presto, a little quick ; poco a poco, little by little.

POLONAISE, a term applied to a peculiar kind of music, always written in ¾ time. See page 196.

PORTAMENTO, mostly used to describe a certain sliding or carrying of the voice from one tone to another.

POSTLUDE, a short section after the main composition.

POTPOURRI, a fanciful composition introducing several airs, usually well known, with variations.

PRELUDE, a preparatory section to the main composition.

PREPARATION, making use of a tone of the same pitch as the dissonant tone of a dissonant chord, in the chord which immediately precedes it.

PRESTO, very quick.

PRESTISSIMO, extremely quick.

PRIMO, 1 mo., first.

PROGRESSION, the process of passing from one tone or chord to another.

QUASI, in the style of; as andante quasi allegretto, andante in the style of allegretto.

RALLENTANDO, RAL., } gradually slower.
RITARDANDO, RITENUTO, RIT., }

RECITATIVE, a kind of vocal music without the usual rhythmic rules, where words are rather recited than sung. Accompanied recitation, one in which some rhythmical regularity is observed.

REPEAT, dots. (:) when placed before a bar thus, ( :‖) they indicate a repetition of the preceding section. When placed after a bar thus, (‖: ) they indicate a repetition of the following section.

RESOLUTION, The progression of any chord but a common chord, or either of its tones, to a different one.

REST, a character indicating a certain duration of silence. The following are the rests in common use : ▬ whole rest ; ▬ half rest ; ♪ or ♪ quarter rest : ♪ eighth rest ; ♪ sixteenth rest ; ♪ thirty-second rest. (There may be also a dotted and double dotted rest of each kind.) Each rest corresponds in its length to the note of like name.

R. H., right hand.

RHYTHMICS, the name of the department in music that treats of the length of tones. The following are the names of the principal things belonging to it : notes, rests, dots, measures, parts of measures, beats, counting, bars, movement, including adagio, allegro, ritard, &c.

SCALE, a series of tones in a certain order. Major scale a series of eight tones named as to their relative pitch, one, two, three, four, five, six, seven and eight. This, when given successively from one to eight, produces the following order of intervals, step, step, half step, step, step, step, half step. Harmonic minor scale, a series of eight tones named as the major, one two three, &c., which when given successively from one to eight, produces the following order of intervals, step, half step, step, step, half step, step and a half, half step. Melodic minor scale, a series of eight tones named as the harmonic, which when given as before, produces successively the following; step, half step, step step, step, step, half step. In descending, this scale unlike the others, has different tones, and a corresponding difference in the order of its intervals. They are as follows : step, step, half step, step, step, half step, step. There are other minor scales, but these are the most common. The three scales above mentioned, are called diatonic. Chromatic scale, a series of thirteen tones, which, when given successively from lowest to highest, or vice versa, produce, only half steps. · This scale is named as to relative pitch, one, sharp one, two, sharp two, &c., or descending eight, seven, flat seven, six, flat six, &c. It may here be said that a major and a minor scale or key having the same signature, are called relative to each other : as for example, the scale or key of C major is said to be the relative major to the scale or key of A minor, and vice versa.

SCORE, all the parts of a vocal or instrumental composition.

SECOND, the interval made by a tone and the next one to it in the order of a diatonic scale.

SECTION, one of the larger divisions of a piece of music.

SEGNO, SEG., ⸹ sign.

SEGUE, SEGUITO, now follows, as *segue il coro*, the chorus now follows. It is also used to show that a subsequent passage is to be performed like that which precedes it.

SEMPRE, SEM., all the way, as *sempre legato*, all the way legato.

SEMPLICE, (CON,) with simplicity.

SENZA, without, as *senza replica*, without repetition.

SEQUENCE, a succession of similar chords or intervals in a uniform manner.

SEVENTH, the interval made by a tone and the next one to it but five in the order of a diatonic scale.

SFORZANDO, sf. sfz. See FORZANDO.

SHAKE, see trill.

SHARP, the name of a character (♯) that is used to make a line or space of the staff indicate a pitch a half step higher than it would if there were no character but the clef upon it.

SHARP FOURTH, a fourth consisting of three steps.

SIGNATURE, one, two, three or more sharps or flats (and sometimes naturals) placed upon the staff at the commencement of a piece or section of music, to make the staff indicate the right pitch for the key in which the piece is to be performed. For example, the key of D major, consists of the tones A, B, C sharp, D, E, F sharp and G. The staff with only the clef upon it, indicates the pitch of the tones A, B, C, D, E, F, and G, which make the key of C. By placing sharps upon those degrees of the staff that usually stand for the pitches of F, and C, their signification is changed, and they are made to stand for the pitches F sharp and C sharp, and the sharps so placed form the signature or sign of the key.

SIMILE, similarly, in like manner.

SIXTH, the interval made by a tone and the next but four to it in the order of a diatonic scale.

SMORZANDO, SMORZATO, SMORZ, dying away.

SOLFEGGIO, melodious kind of exercise for the voice, see page 124.

SONATA, a composition consisting of several movements, generally for a single instrument with or without accompaniment.

SOSTENUTO, SOST., sustained.

SOTTO VOCE, softly, subdued, in an undertone.

SPACES, certain degrees of the staff.

STACCATO, the style of performing music in which each tone is made very short, and as much detached from the others as the time will admit, also the name of the character (') that indicates this style. Used to avoid multiplying the rests and the more unusual notes.

STAFF, the character used to represent the pitch of tones. The staff consists of lines and spaces, each of which, is called a degree. There are, or may be, as many degrees in the staff as there are pitches of tones in any key. Only eleven of these degrees (five lines and six spaces,) are usually printed in full; when others are wanted, they are temporarily added by means of short lines.

STEP, an interval as large as two half steps—steps and half steps are used in analyzing scales and larger intervals.

STRAIN, a line or section of music.

STRINGENDO, accelerating the movement.

SUBDOMINANT, the name in harmony, sometimes given to four of a diatonic scale.

SUBMEDIANT, the name in harmony some times given to six of a diatonic scale.

SUBTONIC, the name in harmony sometimes given to seven of a diatonic scale.

SUSPENSION, an accented tone not belonging to the chord with which it is given. See page 106.

SUPERTONIC, the name in harmony sometimes given to two of a diatonic scale.

SYMPHONY, the highest kind of instrumental composition.

SYNCOPATION, when a tone commences on an unaccented part of a measure and continues through an accented part, it is called a syncopation. When a tone commences on the last half of one part of a measure and continues through the first half of the next part, a similar effect is produced, and the same name is given to it. A well given syncopated tone is always accented.

TASTO SOLO, T. S., a term used to indicate that the other parts are to cease, and the base to be played.

TEMPO, TEM., time. *Tempo primo* is equivalent to *a tempo*, which see.

TENTH, an interval of an octave and a third.

TENUTO, TEN., the tenacious of; hold the tone to its fullest extent.

TERZA, the interval of a third.

THEME, The melody in certain kinds of music, on which as a text the other sections are composed.

THIRD, the interval made by a tone and the next but one to it in the order of the diatonic scale.

THOROUGH BASE, playing through the base by means of figures.

TIE, The name of a character like a legato mark, but used only over or under two notes on the same degree of the staff to make them stand for one tone.

TIME, A word which in music not only has its usual signification, but also means movement, and sometimes measure, as double time, &c.

TONE, a musical sound, the essential properties of which are length, pitch and power. In written music the property of length is represented by a note, the property of pitch by a line or space of the staff, and the property of power by some dynamic term or sign either expressed or understood, and the combination of all stands for a tone. It is hardly necessary to add that if either of these properties be taken away from a tone it ceases to exist, and that no representation of a tone is perfect that does not provide for the representation of these three properties. See definition of note, staff, and dynamics. Tones are named as to their length by the names of notes. They are named as to their absolute pitch by the names of the first seven letters of the alphabet, with, in some cases, the addition of the words flat, sharp, natural, double flat or double sharp, large, small, once marked, twice marked, &c. They are named as to their relative pitch by some of the names of numbers. They are named as to their proper by the terms and names in the department of Dynamics. The diagram on page 18 shows the representations of tones as to their pitch and gives their exact names. It will be seen that the tone so well known as middle C is also named *once marked small C*. The tone a half step above that, is named either once marked C sharp, or once marked small D flat, and so of other intermediate tones. This representation might easily extend so as to include all the tones that the ear can appreciate.

TONIC, the name in harmony sometimes given to one, or the key note of a diatonic scale.

TRANSPOSITION, playing or singing a scale, exercise, or tune, in a higher or lower key.

TREMOLO, TREMANDO, TREM., tremulously. See page 219.

TRILL, The rapid alternation of two contiguous tones. See page 195.

TRIO, a piece of music, in three parts; also the second movement in certain kinds of music which leads to the performance again of the first section or movement.

TRIPLET, see definition of note.

TROPPO, too much.

TUTTA, all, *con tutta la forza*, with all the force.

TUTTI, all the voices or instruments, or both.

UN., a or an; as *un poco*, a little.

UNA CORDA, one string; applicable to pianos whose softer tones may be produced by making the hammers strike one string. Equivalent to piano or *p*.

UNISON, produced by two or more tones of the same pitch.

VELOCE, or *con velocita*, with velocity.

VIVACE, VIVO, with vivacity.

VOCE, voice; *voce di petto*, chest voice; *voce di testa*, head voice.

VOLTI SUBITO, V. S., turn the leaf quickly.

# THE MUSICAL CURRICULUM.

———————✦———————

To the Pupil.—I write over the lessons the substance of what your teacher will be likely to tell you in the course of his instructions. This is done that you may not forget important directions, while you are practicing by yourself; for bad habits are formed or kept up by forgetting or neglecting such directions, and good ones are acquired only by constantly observing them. You will therefore do well to read over these hints and directions, and to look at the cuts that illustrate good positions, every time you sit down to practice, and continue to do this until good habits in all things are formed.  G. F. R.

**No. 1.** Position. Letters as names of Tones. (See page 3.)
Take your place before the center of the key-board. Have the seat so high that the point of the elbows shall fall a trifle below the surface of the keys, and let the elbows be as far forward as the front of the shoulder. Strike all the C's upon the piano, also all the D's and all the G's.

**No. 2.** Intervals, on the Piano and on the Hands.
Play seconds, thirds, fourths and fifths, all over the key-board, with each hand—reckoning them both upward and downward—using white keys only.

**No. 3.** Quarter Notes. Staff. Treble Clef. Places on the Staff representing middle C, and the D next above it. Intervals on the Staff. Marks of Fingering.
Right Hand.—Keep the hand still. Do not leave one key down while striking the next. Name the interval that occurs here.

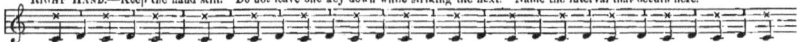

**No. 4.** Base Clef. The C next below middle C, and the G next below that.
Left Hand.—Do not tip the hand sidewise. Observe the other directions. Strike with the thumb and finger only. Hold the hand perfectly square and still, as if a glass of water stood on it that you dare not spill.

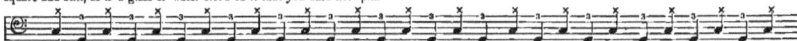

**No. 5.** Brace. Measures. Double Time. Figures. Bars. Counting. Double Bars.
Both Hands.—Hands and body in good position and still. Keep the eyes upon the notes. Play steadily and slow. Observe the intervals to be played, on the piano and on the staff, and let those of your hand correspond.

**No. 6.** The same lesson an octave higher. Middle C in the Base.
Always keep the same place exactly before the center of the key-board, unless you are playing in a four-hand piece. Observe that the left hand now commences with middle C, and the right hand with the C next above it, or an octave higher.

**No. 7.** Half Note. Accent. Moderato. Metronome Marks.

Find your place by the middle C. Do not count faster at the half notes. Do not sing the counts, but speak them promptly and steadily. Strike on the *ends* of the fingers, but on the *sides* of the thumbs. Take pattern from the little sketch at the commencement of this Lesson. Name the intervals that occur here. What indicates the pitch of these tones? What their length?

*Moderato.*   ♩=104.

**No. 8.** E in the Treble. Mezzo and Forte, and their Abbreviations. Tie.

Keep the thumb over the keys while the fingers are playing. Observe the expression—Medium and Loud. When there is no mark indicating movement, *Moderato* is to be understood. What interval is indicated at the third and fourth notes of the treble here? What is a third below the second finger of the right hand?

**No. 9.** Triple Measure. Dotted Half Notes. Expression invented by the Pupil.

When there are no marks of expression, such as *Mezzo* or *Forte*, exercise your own taste—make the lesson sound as well as possible. Move fingers only. It will not take long to form good habits, if you do not forget and let the bad ones come in and rule.

**No. 10.** F in Treble. B in Base.

Play the lesson is perfect; then give it the time indicated by *Moderato*. Count steadily through the dotted half-notes. Name the sounds indicated by the degrees of the staff while pointing at the lines and spaces, before playing the lesson: as C, D, E, &c. Do this frequently for a few days, or until you become familliar with them.

**No. 11.** A in Base. Quarter Rest.

Play the lesson so slow that you can make it perfect in regard to striking the right keys the first time you try it. This will be done by reckoning the intervals in the lesson and at the fingers as you play—a process, slow at first, after a while accomplished at a glance.

**No. 12. G in Treble. Quadruple Measure. Whole Note.**

Do not tip the hand sidewise—keep it level. Observe expression. Avoid all grimaces and distortions. Do not look on your hands. Keep the fingers on the right keys by observing the intervals as they occur. Make the fingers strike like little hammers. Do not let the finger nails touch the keys. Observe carefully and imitate closely the position of the hand in this sketch, especially of the finger that is raised to strike; and let each finger assume the same position as it is raised. The thumb is raised without curving.

**No. 13. F in Base.**

Keep the thumb of the right hand over C. All care that you bestow at this stage of your practice, will strengthen the foundation on which to build a beautiful superstructure. When the marks of expression are not given, try experiments until the different degrees of strength are so used as to make the lesson sound well.

**No. 14. Piano, and its Abbreviation. Half Rest.**

Find your place by middle C. Do not strike the little finger on its side. Look quiet and pleasant. After you have learned this lesson so that it will go through in time and tune, play it once applying the same degree of strength to every part of it; then play it according to the dynamic marks, and observe the difference.

**No. 15. (Learn No. 16 next after this. It will be found on page 45.)**

Do not move the hand around. Move fingers only. Name the tones and intervals before playing the lesson. Review carefully every day. Remember that a lesson to benefit you must be learned. A lesson is not learned because you can play it once through without making a mistake. It only becomes learned and settled by reviewing it day after day for several days.

**No. 17. Change of Position.**

Do not strike the little finger of the left hand on its side. In the base of this lesson there is an excellent opportunity to notice and practice all the intervals you have had. Do not consider it learned until you can play it without looking at your hands; and think, while you play, what interval you are making, and also the names of the tones you produce.

**No. 18.** Change of Position of Right Hand.

Observe that the hands are now changing their position, so as to bring other tones into the field. Notice the different effects of the music in the different positions. Try to keep in mind the names of the tones, also the intervals on the hands as well as the notes. Do not look down.

**No. 19.** Change of Position. Beginning on last part of Measure.

Reckon intervals carefully until you can tell them at a glance. Go slow and sure. Do not hollow in the fingers at the ends, but let them curve outward as shown in the plate of correct position. Bring out all the meaning there may be in these lessons. This effort will improve your taste.

**No. 20.** Change of Position. Section. Repeat.

Play each part alone first, so that when you put them together they may be as nearly as possible perfect the first time through. Do not sing or drawl the counts, any more than you would move your hand sluggishly if you were beating time.

## "O MUSIC, SWEET MUSIC."

**No. 21.** Change of Position of Right Hand. Singing.

Let the principal effort in singing be directed to keeping in exact tune with the piano, and in giving out the voice freely and naturally. Although we do not commence the study of singing yet, you may make this little song sound as well as you can.

O mu - sic, sweet mu - sic, thy prai - ses we will sing. And tell of the pleas - ure and joy that thou dost bring. At

morn - ing and eve - ning and in the si - lent night, O mu - sic, sweet mu - sic thou art my heart's de - light.

**No. 22.**     **THE FIRST DUET.**---Secondo.

In playing the second of four-hand pieces, sit opposite the center of the lower half of the piano. Remember to have the intervals on the hand correspond to those on the staff. Do not let the wrist fall below the knuckles. Do not let the finger nails strike the keys.

**THE FIRST DUET.**---Primo.

**No. 23. Change of Position. Treble Clef for Left Hand.**

To play this lesson sit opposite the center of the upper half of the piano. This and No. 22 may be played together. Observe that the right hand commences two octaves above middle C, and the left hand one octave above it.

**No. 24. F Sharp. Key Note G. Signature.**

Find your place by middle C. Play F sharp instead of F. Each two degrees of the staff that are next to each other represent a second—whatever tones they stand for. So F sharp is a second from E, or from G: and on the piano it is not only a second from E to F, but from E to F sharp; not only a second from F to G, but from F sharp to G; and a third from F sharp to A, and so on.

**No. 25. Sextuple Measure. Dotted Whole Note.**

The place on the staff which sometimes represents F, now represents F sharp. F would not sound well. Name intervals, and think of them while you play. Be determined, from the beginning, to *understand music*—to know the structure and meaning of that which you play and sing, as well as you do the story you read.

**No. 26.**

You will probably incline to strike the little finger on its side. Avoid it, and get the hand settled into a good position as soon as possible. If every step be well taken, there will be no greater difficulty at the middle or end of the book, when you get there, than you find here.

**No. 27. Andantino.**

Make the melody *sing* as much as you can, but do not sing yourself. Remember that your musical perception, or ear, can be improved as well as your fingers—as can also your taste and appreciation.

### WELCOME, HOUR OF SONG.

**No. 28.** (You will find No. 29 on page 46.)

While you are singing, observe all the things necessary to playing well. Do not hold the hand stiff. Let the strength come from the fingers alone. Right lessons and pieces well learned, although simple, will give pleasure to yourself and friends at every step, while at the same time they are exercising and developing all your musical powers.

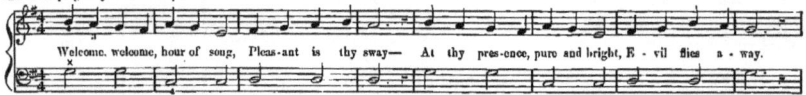

Welcome, welcome, hour of song, Pleas-ant is thy sway— At thy pres-ence, pure and bright, E - vil flies a - way.

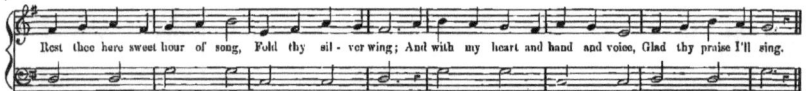

Rest thee here sweet hour of song, Fold thy sil - ver wing; And with my heart and hand and voice, Glad thy praise I'll sing.

## THE SECOND DUET.---Secondo.

**No. 30.** Base Clef in upper Staff.

Agree with your companion where you will play *loud* and *soft*. Play sometimes 1st, and sometimes 2d. If you are so far along, in your appreciation of music, that these lessons seem to you more adapted for younger persons, you should remember that we must become "as little children" to learn any thing well. There is no such thing as beginning with grown up music.

## THE SECOND DUET.---Primo.

**No. 31.**

May be played with No. 30. Practice each lesson thoroughly, whether played as duet or not. Keep trying to hit the right note without looking, and try also to have the intervals in your mind as you play, without the apparent effort of thinking—both will come after a moderate amount of effort.

**No. 32.** C Sharp. Key Note D.

Find your place by middle C. Hands still—eyes upon notes. F sharp and C sharp, instead of F and C, to make the key note right. You should be able to touch the right keys without looking, as unerringly as you can your mouth, eyes or forehead. Try to feel that you make the fingers move from the knuckles, without moving the other joints.

**No. 33.**      **"OVER THE MEADOWS."**

When you can play and sing these lessons readily, notice whether you take your breath between the syllables. Do not sing the piece until you can play it quite easily. Pay constant attention to the correct position of the hands, so that the minute you place them over the key-board they will take the right position. *Now* is the time to do this, as you will soon have other things to attend to, and the hand will be left to take care of itself.

O - ver the mead-ows so pear - ly, Soft - ly the breez - es stray, Bear-ing the song of the

wild - bird, Far to the woodlands a - way.... A - way! a - way! a - way!... Far to the woodlands a - way....

**No. 34. Marcato. Crescendo, and its Abbreviation.**

Take the finger or thumb off the "marcato" notes neatly by lifting the hand, as in the cut on next page. Remember that learning the notes here is but *beginning* this lesson — ease, facility and good expression must follow to complete it.

**No. 35.**      **THE THIRD DUET.**---Secondo.

You observe that the thumbs strike the first notes. Let the thought of the intervals in the music, and on the fingers, guide you. Think also, if possible, of the names of the tones.

## THE THIRD DUET.---Primo.

**No. 36.** (No. 37 is on page 46.)

Find your place by middle C. Agree with your companion about expression. If you learn the lesson in the book imperfectly, or more especially if you seek others, out of it, that are not suited to you, you will dread to play or sing when asked, and give little or no pleasure when you do. You may persist in this course, thinking you will learn after a while, but that is a delusion, and like the Jack o'-lantern, will lead you into quagmires and impenetrable thickets of difficulty. *Only* those pieces that you can perform to any body, and at any time, are right ones for you.

**No. 38. G Sharp. Key Note A.**

You will now find F sharp, C sharp, and G sharp necessary to make the lesson sound well, and to make the key-note A. Name the tones and intervals the first thing, and think of them as you play. Overcome each difficulty thoroughly, that you may be prepared to meet the next.

**No. 39. Da Capo. Fine.**

Are you becoming confirmed in a good position of the hands? Remember that playing *fast* is not playing *well*. To read well, look a little ahead of where you are playing, that you may not be taken by surprise. The cut above is to show how the hand is raised *after* striking the marcato notes.

**No. 40.** Allegretto.

If you make mistakes, it will probably be because you are playing too fast. A good plan, under such circumstances, is to commence again, and go just half as fast. A piece that has some places in it that you can not get right, or that by great labor and care and the most favorable circumstances, you can just get through in time and tune, without expression, is *not suited* to you, and will give no pleasure to tasteful people. Neatness, ease and finish, in a performance, are much more agreeable than the appearance of difficulty; so do not be anxious to play or sing music too difficult for you, but rather strive to give with finish and elegance that which is adapted to your present condition and attainments.

*(musical notation)*

**No. 41.**　　"I LOVE THE GLEAMS OF SUN-LIGHT."

Attend to names of tones, intervals, right positions, and good expression. What, taken with G sharp, will make a second? A third? A fourth? What, taken with C sharp, will make those intervals? What, taken with F sharp, will make them? Reckon both upwards and downwards.

*(musical notation)*

I love the gleams of sun - light At my o - pen door, All flick - 'ring thro' the branch - es, Fall - ing on the floor.

They dance in gay - est meas - ure While my song I sing, O sweet the gleams of sun - light, And the joy they bring.

**No. 42.**　　THE FOURTH DUET.---Secundo.

Do not throw the hand up at the rests, but let it stay quietly in its place until it is wanted again. Count promptly until the piece is learned.

*(musical notation)*

**No. 43.**                    **THE FOURTH DUET.**---Primo.

Endeavor to keep the time perfectly together. Be careful to take off the finger neatly at notes marked marcato. Are you able more quickly to tell the intervals as they occur in the music, and more readily to adopt the corresponding intervals on the hands? Are your hands beginning to assume, as it were of themselves, the right positions when you place them on the keys?

**No. 45.** D Sharp. Key Note E.

Are the fingers striking like little hammers, and without tipping or moving the hand?

**No. 46.**

When the first finger reaches over the thumb to strike the black key, the thumb should roll a little, so that the hand shall not move at the wrist. You observe that the first and second fingers here are obliged to extend themselves so as to make a third.

**No. 47.** Diminuendo, and its Abbreviation.

Do not commence "cres." too loud, nor "dim." too soft. Do not look down to see the key you are going to strike—if necessary, look after you have struck, to see if you have made the right interval. If you make a mistake do not nod your head, or make a face.

**No. 48.** Legato Mark.

Slow at first—allegretto at last. It will not be perfect until you can play it at least three consecutive times without a mistake. Do not let the fingers bend inward when striking the black keys. Remember that the legato mark indicates closely connected tones.

## "BANISH YOUR SADNESS."

**No. 49.** First Time and Second Time.

The words will guide you in regard to the first and second endings.

Ban - ish your sad - ness,    Let naught but glad-ness    Fill ev - ery heart in this pleas - ant hour.
O   do not bor - row    One thought of sor - row.    Yield to the spell of the (omit.............)
                                                            Song - Fai - ry's power.

Come while 'tis o'er us,    Join in the cho - rus,    Yield thee, O yield, to the Song Fai - ry's power.

**No. 51.**                  THE FIFTH DUET.---Secondo.

Are you forming the habit of thinking what tones and intervals you make as you play? Remember that your object is intelligence in regard to all things that you acquire, as well as facility and correctness in execution.

**No. 52.**   THE FIFTH DUET.---Primo.

When two notes have a legato mark over or under them, the indication is that the first receives some accent—that the two tones are connected as much as possible, and that the last is left lightly and neatly—somewhat as if it had the sign of the marcato attached to it. You perceive that this breaks in upon the natural accent of the measure, but that is often set aside for higher expressions. The left hand moves on steadily.

**No. 53. A Sharp. Key Note B.**

Give the expression according to your own taste. Try both loud and soft, for an ending, and see which you like best. Although the fingers are not so much curved when striking the black keys as when striking the white ones, still they should not be straight.

**No. 54.**

The black keys accommodate the inequalities of the fingers. Put the first finger over the thumb with as little motion of the hand as possible.

**No. 56. E Sharp. Key Note F Sharp.**

Observe that E sharp is the same as F. Remember that the cut above is only to show how the hand looks after leaving a marcato note.

**No. 58. B Sharp. Key Note C Sharp.**

Observe that B sharp is the same as C. Every tone is a half-step higher than if the key-note were C.

**No. 60.** Key Note C. The Interval of the Sixth..
We commence again with our first key. Can you play any of the preceding lessons without a mistake? It will be unwise to go on until you can.

**No. 61.** You observe that in these lessons there is a new interval, (the sixth,) and that the fingers must be a little extended to reach it.

**No. 62.** Play so slow that you can make the lesson perfect in regard to striking the right keys the first time you try it.

**No. 63.** This is an important movement. Become perfectly familiar with it. When there are no marks of expression, supply them yourself, after finding out what sounds best. To do this try various ways of applying the dynamic degrees.

**No. 64.** It will be necessary to become so familiar with this sixth that you will not only recognise it at a glance, but that the hands will play it accurately without the aid of the eyes.

**No. 65. B Flat. Key Note F.**
Develop what expression there may be in every unmarked lesson. Be careful when striking the little finger not to let it lie straight, but strike with the end, and do not let the hand turn on one side.

**No. 66. Eighth Notes.** "SING, BROTHERS, SING!"
Do not prolong the counts in a singing tone. Speak them promptly. Try to play the sixths in the base neatly and accurately, without looking down.

Sing, brothers, sing; Sing, brothers, sing; Time's on the wing, Time's on the wing, Bear-ing a - way Hopes that to - day Close round the young spir - it cling,
Yes, brothers, sing; Yes, brothers, sing; Time's on the wing, Time's on the wing, Still af - ter night Cum - eth the light— And af - ter win - ter the spring;

But do not sigh That thus they fly, Oth - ers will come When they are gone. Sing, brothers, sing; Sing, brothers sing; While time is fly - ing a - long,
So do not grieve, Sor - rows will leave When comes the day With cheering ray. Yes, brothers, sing; Yes, brothers sing; The' time is fly - ing a - way.

**No. 67.** If you have formed good habits, your left hand will be very quiet in this lesson. You can apply the words which are set to the previous melody to this, after you have learned it. Notice that the eighth notes do not all look alike. It is convenient often to join them together in a group by the mark which makes them eighths. Do not begin the crescendos too loud, nor the diminuendos too soft.

**No. 69.**  Remember to review the number of lessons that your teacher gives you, leaving off one as you learn one.

**No. 70.**  **THE SIXTH DUET.**---Secondo.
Accent and connect according to the legato marks.  See that no bad habit, with regard to position, is quietly fastening itself upon you.

**No. 71.**  **THE SIXTH DUET.**---Primo.
Make yourself familiar with distinguishing the added lines and spaces quickly.  Keep the fingers properly curved.

No. 72. E Flat. Key Note B Flat. Syncopation.
Observe the accent required by the syncopation. You perceive that accents sometimes fall on parts of the measure usually unaccented.

No. 73. Observe that the same fingers are used for different groups of notes. Give a neat accent at the beginning of the legato marks.

No. 74.                         THE SEVENTH DUET.---Second.
Think, as you play, of names of tones, intervals, dynamic degrees, expression, position of hands, and movements of fingers.

                        THE SEVENTH DUET.---Primo.
No. 75. Appoggiatura.

## "SWIFTLY O'ER THE TIDE."

**No. 76.**  Practice as carefully and diligently as if your teacher's eyes were upon you.  He can only guide and aid you—he can not learn for you.

1. Swift-ly o'er the tide,   Fai-ry   lit-tle  May, My dar-ling May,      In our boat we glide, Fai-ry   lit-tle
2. On our light bark flies, Fai-ry   lit-tle  May, My dar-ling May,      With the breeze she vies, Fai-ry   lit-tle

May, My   dar-ling May.      Spark-ling  in  our path-way See the mer-ry,  mer-ry  rip-ples play, As  we
May, My   dar-ling May.      Spark-ling  as  we pass them, Still the mer-ry, mer-ry  rip-ples play, And we

sing  our  joy-ous  song. Fai-ry  lit-tle  May, My  dar-ling May—        May,  dar-ling  May.
sing  our  joy-ous  song. Fai-ry  lit-tle  May, My  dar-ling May—        May,  dar-ling  May.

**No. 77.**  Do not allow yourself in any unusual motion or grimace when you happen to make a mistake.  Preserve your self-possession.

**No. 78.**  Holding down one key while striking the next is one of the greatest enemies to neat and tasteful playing; and yet each note should have its full time.

**No. 80. A Flat. Key Note E Flat.**
Overcome the new difficulties thoroughly. Do not forget to keep the key and the intervals in mind.

**No. 81.** You will never become a good player without being a correct timist. Counting aloud will help you in this.

cres............ dim......................

cres................dim......... cres...............................dim...........................

**No. 82.** **"SITTING ROUND THE HEARTH-STONE."**

Sit - ting round the hearth-stone When the day is o'er, Think-ing of the dear ones On the dis-tant shore.

Sing-ing as we pon-der, Of their home so fair, Sigh-ing-ly we mur-mur, "Shall we know them there."

G

**No. 83.**    THE EIGHTH DUET.---Secondo.

When you have learned to play your lesson through without mistakes, you are then just ready to practice it with most profit.

**No. 84.**    THE EIGHTH DUET.---Primo.

Remember you are to learn to make a *correct* player. That is *your* part of the work. The fast playing will come of itself.

**No. 85.**  Varieties of Measure. Dotted Quarter Note. Dal Segno.

It is hoped that you will find the pieces here attractive enough to yourself and your friends, to prevent you from urging your teacher out of the regular course to get other music. You can count six in this measure, or two.

**No. 87.  D Flat.  Key Note A Flat.**
Do your hands take the right position without thought on your part?  If so, that good habit is formed.

**No. 88.**  Keep both hands well over the black keys.  Remember that the expression is just as important as the time and tune.

## "MERRILY OVER THE WATER."

**No. 89.  Eighth Rests.**
Give the right pronunciation to the second syllables of "merrily" and "cheerily."

Mer - ri - ly o - ver the wa - ter, Mer - ri - ly, mer - ri - ly oh!  Cheer - i - ly on we are row - ing, Cheeri - ly, cheer-i - ly,

oh!  Keep-ing the time with our voi - ces, True to the dip of the oar.  Mer - ri - ly on we are fly - ing,

Mer - ri - ly on to the shore.  Mer - ri - ly on we are fly - ing, Mer - ri - ly on to the shore.

**No. 90.**  THE NINTH DUET.---Secondo.
Put the right arm over the left of the one who plays the primo.

**No. 91.**  THE NINTH DUET.---Primo.
Do not count faster at the rests.  Leave the notes neatly.

**No. 93.**  G Flat.  Key Note D Flat.
After playing this, play No. 58, and notice in what respects they differ, and in what respects they are alike.

**No. 95.**  C Flat.  Key Note G Flat.
After playing this, play No. 56.  Do not neglect the five finger exercises, but practice them in their order.

**No. 97.**  F Flat.  Key Note C Flat.
Every tone a half-step lower than when the key-note is C.  After playing this, play No. 53.

**No. 99.** Give a little accent to the first note of each group in the base, and to the first note of each legato mark in the treble; also let the last note of each group and of each legato mark be light. The hand must be somewhat independent to do this, as you perceive.

## FIVE-FINGER EXERCISES.

These exercises, technically called "five-finger exercises," are for the fingers what gymnastic and calisthenic exercises are for the rest of the body, and should, like them, be practiced every day; as it is only in this way that muscular improvement can be made. Although not learned at once, these lessons are printed together, that time may not be lost in searching for them in various parts of the book. Until you have played to No. 16, this work will not commence—after that add them as you learn them, in the order of their numbers, to the list of things to be done first in each day's practice. The one without a number, your teacher will show you how to use. It will be awkward to the untrained muscles, but should be persisted in until it is thoroughly mastered, and the fingers become readily subservient to the will. As you acquire legato, marcato, crescendo, diminuendo, and other styles, apply them, a part of the time, in the practice of these exercises.

Each two measures should be practiced until the fingers begin to grow tired, and no longer.

**No. 16.** Five Finger Exercise in C. If you practice two hours a day, the first half hour should be given to these exercises.

**No. 29.** Five Finger Exercise in G.   Be as careful as possible about position of hands and movement of fingers.

**No. 37.** Five Finger Exercise in D.   Introduce here such expression as you are acquiring in the other lessons.

**No. 44.** Five Finger Exercise in A.   Notice the intervals that occur in the music, and see that the hands correspond.

**No. 50.** Five Finger Exercise in E.   Ask yourself, for each of the exercises, what key it is in.

**No. 55.** Five Finger Exercise in B.   Play slow enough to be exact in time and graceful in execution.

**No. 57.** Five Finger Exercise in F Sharp.   Strike the black keys evenly and surely. Fingers not so much curved.

**No. 59.** Five Finger Exercise in C Sharp.   Be careful, in this exercise, not to strike two keys at a time.

No, 68. Five Finger Exercise. Key of F. Learn every piece in the book, in the order of its number.

No. 70. Five Finger Exercise. Key of B Flat. Keep the hand well over the black keys. Do not strike two keys at once

No. 86. Five Finger Exercise. Key of E Flat. Strike up as well as down. Let the fingers leave the keys with a prompt movement.

No. 92. Five Finger Exercise. Key of A Flat. If you make mistakes, you are playing too fast. Begin again, and play half as fast.

No. 94. Five Finger Exercise. Key of D Flat. Remember the cuts illustrating good positions, and play with even, graceful motion.

No. 96. Five Finger Exercise. Key of G Flat. See that the wrist does not rise and fall at each stroke of the fingers.

No. 98. Five Finger Exercise. Key of C Flat. No one has ever become a good pianist without practicing five finger exercises.

**No. 100.** Staccato.     **THE TENTH DUET.**---Secondo.

Before playing this lesson, exercise each finger in succession, on any key of the pianoforte, producing staccato tones. Notice the position, before striking, as illustrated by Fig. 1, and after striking, as illustrated by Fig. 2.

**No. 101.**     **THE TENTH DUET.**---Primo.

The half notes are not staccato, but are held their full time. The others have a short, sharp, sudden stroke, making the tone like a point. Observe that the stroke is given by *drawing off* the finger, or the thumb.

**No. 102.**   Let the hand remain as quiet while producing the staccato tones, as is consistent with a quick, springy movement of the fingers.

**No. 103.** Be careful to draw off the finger in the right manner to produce the staccato—also make the short tone light. Observe that where the last note of a legato mark is two or more counts long, it is not made staccato.

**No. 104.** Give this expression according to your own taste. Make the legato tones sing. Do not let the staccato tones be coarse or too abrupt. It is hoped that the intervals as far as the sixth are now familiar, and that they can be named and played without the least hesitation.

**No. 105.** While the left hand plays steadily, making only the usual variations of soft and loud, the right hand should give the accent which commences the legato phrase, and the delicate staccato tone which closes it, connecting the two tones closely together. After practicing these staccato lessons, play your five finger exercises, staccato, at least once each day for several days.

**No. 106.** Cadence. Transposition.

The transposition of this cadence is here printed in full, that you may see as well as hear its beautiful order. In the study of harmony, if you speak of an interval—a fifth for example—it is always understood to mean a fifth *upward*, unless otherwise expressly stated; so that in speaking of the fifth from C, G would be meant, although you may find it a *fourth below*. Therefore the transposition through the keys, in this way, is said to be a transposition by FIFTHS. Notice that the cadence in F♯ and G♭ are the same to the ear, differing only in representation. Notice also that, from that point, the transposition, although still by fifths, and the same to the ear, is indicated by one less character in the signature each time, instead of one more—taking away a flat producing the same effect as adding a sharp.

Play this cadence in the different keys as written, and also in the following order, viz: C, F, B♭, E♭, A♭, D♭, G♭, F♯, B, E, A, D, G, and C. This you see is going back again, and is a transposition by fourths.

**No. 107.** Play this cadence in all the keys, transposing first by fifths, then again by fourths. The intervals in the right hand being seconds, there will be but little difficulty when you get started on the right key-note, though you must remember that there is no F when the key-note is G; and neither F nor C when the key-note is D; but F sharp, C sharp, and so on. In the base, you will notice that you first go down a fifth from the key-note, then up a second, then up a fourth. Your knowledge of intervals will be serviceable to you here.

**No. 108.** Play and sing this little phrase of greeting in all the keys, transposing as before, by fifths, (C, G, D, A, E, B, F♯, G♭, D♭, A♭, E♭, B♭, F, and C;) and also by fourths, (C, F, B♭, E♭, A♭, D♭, G♭, F♯, B, E, A, D, G, and C,) thus going around the circle in both directions. Choose the octave which will best accommodate your voice. Do not try to sing too high nor too low. In this lesson are all the intervals that you have practiced. These transpositions should be persisted in until they are familiar, and then should come into your review for several days.

A greet-ing un-to thee,     A greet-ing un-to thee.

A greet-ing un-to thee,     A greet-ing un-to thee.

A greet-ing un-to thee,     A greet-ing un-to thee.

**No. 109.** Transpose this into such keys as your teacher directs. Perhaps you can play it in all the keys, though that would be difficult. You perceive that it is the same tune, wherever you play it, and that transposition is but changing the place as it were of a tune or lesson. Remember that a good practical knowledge of the intervals is of great value in the art of transposition.

* This cadence is printed in G, just to get you started, though you will probably need no assistance. Notice that in the key of G, the base begins an octave higher than it does in the first transposition of No. 106. It does not matter which octave you take. Be careful to choose the best fingering.

**No. 110.** Dotted Quarter Note. Interval of the Seventh.

Do not jerk the eighth notes that follow the dotted quarters. Make them smooth and graceful. Be careful of the place in the left hand where you reach a seventh. Try to get it accurately without looking. Remember not to strike the second of two notes on the same degree of the staff, when they are united by a tie.

**No. 111.** Name the key-note, intervals and movement, and keep in mind all things necessary to an intelligent and tasteful rendering of the piece.

Observe that the letters A, B, C, and D indicate the different exercises of each number. Whatever else you omit to do, make thorough work of these exercises for daily practice, being at the same time systematic and judicious.

**No. 112. A** Transpose this lesson into F.  **B** Transpose to B flat.

Play these lessons thoroughly as written before transposing them.

**No. 113. A** Transpose to E flat.  **B** Transpose to A flat.

Those who find it difficult to sing in tune, or whose voices need flexibility, may sometimes sing these lessons with the piano.

**No. 114. A** Transpose to D flat  **B** Transpose to G flat.

If you sing, you can make use of "ah," or other vowel sounds, or the syllables.

**No. 115. A** Transpose to F sharp  **B** Transpose to B.

Play each lesson accenting the first note in each measure, and then again accenting the second, then the third, and so on.

**No. 116. A**   **B**   **C**   **D**

Transpose to A.  When you accent as directed above, make all but the accented note light.

**No. 117. A**   **B**   **C**   **D**

Transpose to D.  When not accenting as above, give variety, as cres., dim., legato, staccato, &c.

**No. 118. A**   **B**   **C**   **D**

Transpose to G.  If these lessons are not the most interesting in the book, they are among the most important.

**No. 119. A** **B**

Play as written—then transpose a second above.

**No. 120. A** **B** **C** **D**

Transpose a third above.

**No. 121.** Observe that the third measure in each of these exercises is to be played four times. Transpose the lessons a part of the time into the key of 1♭. Hold down the keys indicated by the tied whole notes, but be very careful to hold no others.

**A** **B** **C**

Play this measure four times. FOUR TIMES FOUR TIMES

**No. 122. A** **B** **C**

FOUR TIMES FOUR TIMES FOUR TIMES

**No. 123. A** **B** **C**

FOUR TIMES FOUR TIMES FOUR TIMES

**No. 124. A** **B** **C**

FOUR TIMES FOUR TIMES FOUR TIMES

**No. 125. A** **B** **C**

FOUR FOUR FOUR

## "SOFTLY THE SHADES."

**No. 126.** Double Notes for the Right Hand. Ritard e dim.

Strike these double notes with the hand only—lifting it from the wrist as illustrated by the cut. When the notes succeed each other, as in the third measure, the movement *may* be by the fingers only. Observe that you are now to notice and become familiar with the interval produced by the double notes, as well as those produced by successions.

1. Soft - ly the shades of eve - ning come, Still - ing the gay world's bu - sy hum. No while we sing our
2. Gen - tly the stars gleam in the west, Zeph - yrs have lulled the birds to rest. Plash - ing and cool the

*Ritard e dim.*

last part - ing lay, Slow - ly the day - light fades a - way, Fades a - way, fades a - way.
brook - let at play, Mur - murs be - low, then glides a - way, Glides a - way, glides a - way.

**No. 127.** Double Notes in the Left Hand.

Try the left hand alone until you can strike neatly from the wrist. Notice and name the intervals in the Bass. Look on page 64 for the numbers not found here, and learn them in their order. As they are learned add them to your daily practice.

## "NIGHT'S SHADES NO LONGER."

**No. 130.** Reaching an Octave with the Left Hand.

Notice the key you are in, the names of tones and intervals as you play. Give out the voice freely, and take breath in right places.

1. Night's shades no long - er rest on the land, Bright - ly o'er all doth morn - ing ex - pand— Hail we its
2. What scene so love - ly, what scene so fair, As hill and vale in morn's gold - en air! Wake to their

glo - ries with heart and with voice, Come join in the cho - rus, re - joice, O re - joice.
beau - ties, a - wake heart and voice, Come join in the cho - rus, re - joice, O re - joice.

**No. 132.**   In learning a lesson of any length, do not play the whole of it over and over, but take a few measures and practice until you have learned them well, then a few more, and so on.

BONDO MOVEMENT.

**No. 133.**   Think what intervals the double notes of the right hand make. Strike from the wrist. Left hand smooth and steady.

BONDO MOVEMENT.

## "GAILY THE BRIGHT WINGS."

**No. 134.**   What is the key note here? How are you to strike the double notes? Should you take breath between syllables?

ALLEGRETTO.

1. Gai - ly   the   bright wings are flash - ing,   Out   in   the   mid - sum - mer air,   O - ver   the   flow - ers   so   radiant
2. Wreaths of   rare beau - ty we're twin - ing,   Soon   they   will   grace the sweet bowers—   Oh,   in   the   gar - den   so   fragrant,

Of   the   sweet gar - den   so   fair—   Thou-sands   of bright wings are flash - ing, Out   in   the   gar - den   so   fair.
Swift - ly   fly   mo - ments and hours—   While   the   bright wreaths we   are twin - ing, Swift - ly   fly   mo - ments and hours.

**No. 136.**  Do not count faster at the easy places, but be sure to count so slowly, all through the piece, that you will go steadily through the hard places without stumbling or retarding the time.

RONDO MOVEMENT.

**No. 137.**  Adhere carefully to the fingering.  Do not begin the crescendos too loud, nor the diminuendos too soft.

SLOW WALTZ MOVEMENT.

**No. 138.**  Do not hold the keys down where there are rests.  Let the hand strike up as well as down where the eighth notes are.  What interval prevails in the right hand?

QUICK-STEP MOVEMENT.

**No. 140.**  Notice intervals—make right movements of hands.  Leave notes before rests neatly.
ACCOMPANIMENT FORM.

**No. 141.**     **"WHERE SWEETEST FLOWERS GROW."**
Play these lessons carefully and thoroughly before singing them.  Be careful not to play and sing faster and faster.  (No 142 next.)

1. Where sweet-est flow - ers  grow,   O  list!   list!   list!  And zeph-yrs murmur  low,   O  list!   list!   list!   I
2. Thy pres-ence here we  greet.   O  stay!   stay!   stay!  Thou queen of flow - ers  sweet,   O  stay!   stay!   stay!  And

hear    her     step    so   light    and    free—    And, Oh, what peace and joy   sho brings    to    me.
wear    the    crown    of   sum  -  mer   fair,   Bright Flo-ra, with thy smiles  and sun  -  ny   hair.

**No. 143.**  Observe here that the staccato and also the marcato will require that both hands be lifted alike, although double notes in the left and single notes in the right.  Keep the right hand still at the legato marks, and move it laterally only, at the scales.  When two figures are given for one note, you are at liberty to take either fingering.  At the first note of this number use "2" at commencing, and "x" after D. C.
WALTS MOVEMENT.

**No. 144.**          **THE TWO FRIENDS POLKA.**---(ELEVENTH DUET—Secondo.)

If the hand is not large enough to strike an octave, omit the upper note.    Is there any other interval than the third in the treble?

**No. 146.**          **THE TWO FRIENDS POLKA.**---(ELEVENTH DUET—Primo.)

What key is this piece in?    What kind of time?    What movement has it?    Have you practiced No. 145?

**No. 147.**    In the first and second measures do not move the hand—in the others, only from the wrist.

**No. 149. Enharmonic Change.**

You perceive that the only difference between this and No. 147, is in the representation.

**No. 151.**

**No. 153.**  In this lesson the hands may not be inclined, at first, to go well together.  If this is the case, practice them separately and the whole lesson afterwards measure by measure.

QUICK-STEP MOVEMENT.

**No. 154.**  Give a little accent to the beginning of the measure, but not too much.  Let the power of the accent vary with loud, medium and soft.

WALTZ MOVEMENT.

**No. 156.**  If you wish to learn to play more rapidly, practice the lessons slowly and steadily, and they will seem to come right of themselves.  If you attempt to hurry them, they will become irregular, and you will be apt to make mistakes that it will take you a long time to correct.  In the eighth measure let the first finger strike, then slip the thumb in its place, without letting up on the key.

WALTZ MOVEMENT.

## "LOOK AWAY TO THE FIELDS."

**No. 157.** It will be a good plan to select from these pieces and songs such as you like, and learn to play them without the notes, that you may play or sing for your friends when asked. No. 158 is on page 65.

1. Look a - way to the fields of the har - vest, See the reap - er a - mid the grain, How it rus - tles and trem - bles be -
2. 'Tis the song of a true heart so hap - py, As he gath - ers the shi-ning store, And he thinks of the soft hour of

fore him, Like the rain rip - ples on the main. And list! He sings, As he sweeps o'er the gold - en plain.
twi-light When the la - bor of day is o'er. And see! He smiles, As his eye seeks the cot - tage door.

**No. 159.** Impress upon your mind the idea that you are striving, by slow and careful practice, to play smoothly and correctly, and you will thus acquire rapidity, together with beauty of execution; whereas if you attempt to carry things by storm, and try to make a rapid player by practicing rapidly, you will probably fail in all of these things.

RONDO MOVEMENT.

**No. 160.** It will require some care to move the fingers only in one hand, and from the wrist with the other, at the same time.

WALTZ MOVEMENT.

**No. 161.**                "RAIN DROPS ARE FALLING."

1. Rain - drops are fall - ing, they pat - ter on the au-tumn leaves; Low winds are sigh - ing a - mid the bare and leaf - less trees.
2. Yet 'tis not drea - ry with - in our qui - et hap - py home, While bright and cheer - y a-round our hearth the evenings come.

Gone are all the sweet flowers, and the summer's bright hours Mourn - ful - ly sing in the chill and des - o - lat - ed bowers.
Though we mourn the sweet flowers, au-tumn fruits are now ours— So we will not heed the storm-king's dark and win't'ry powers.

**No. 163.** Practice this lesson at first without accent, or other expression than loud and soft; then practice it giving the proper expression to the legato phrases, syncopations, &c. When learned, the effect should be bright and sparkling, without being very fast.

GALOP MOVEMENT.
ALLEGRETTO.

**No. 164.** Melody and Accompaniment.
You observe that the base has a kind of song to sing. Let it be well connected, and varied as to loud and soft, according to your taste. You will find that, generally, a melody sounds well to be crescendo as it ascends, and diminuendo as it descends.

LEGATO.

**No. 165.**     **"O, HOW SWEET."**

You will observe that a new fingering is introduced here. Be careful to get it well.

1. O how sweet are the echoes at eve-ning, When the vil-lage a-round us is still, Of the shepherd boy's pipe soft-ly
2. And the riv-er be-low gen-tly moan-ing, Hath a charm in the tone of its song, As all dim in the shade of the

peal-ing. As he watch-es his flock on the hill. 'Tis the song of con-tentment and bless-ing, And it spreads far a-way o'er tho
gloam-ing, Its clear wa-ters flow light-ly a-long. How the moon in her splen-dor on ris-ing, Loves to mir-ror her face in the

dale— To the wea-ry it comes with ca-ress-ing, To the sad with a sil-ver-y veil.
deep, While the breez-es with soft ca-dence sigh-ing, Lull the for-est to shad-ow-y sleep.

**No. 167.**   You have probably observed that the principal objects in going through the keys, this time, has been to strike double notes neatly from the wrist, and to play single scales, moving the hand laterally only. If you have not accomplished these objects, you had better by all means review until this is done.

MARCH MOVEMENT.

**No. 168.**   Keep in mind the key, intervals, movements of hands, position, expression, and all things which will make you a thorough and intelligent musician.

WALTZ MOVEMENT.

**No. 169.** THE THREE FRIENDS WALTZ.---(TRIO—Primo.)

This piece will require great exactness in time, pitch and expression, to sound well. The one who plays this part sits at the upper part of the piano.

**No. 170.** THE THREE FRIENDS WALTZ.---(TRIO—Secondo.)

Let the one who plays this part sit opposite the middle of the piano, a little higher than the others. Let the left arm of this player be over the right of the one who plays the third.

**No. 171.** THE THREE FRIENDS WALTZ.---(TRIO—Terzo.)

The player of this part sits at the lower part of the piano. Strike the base pretty firmly. The upper notes of the octave can be omitted. Let the right hand of the one who plays this part be under the left arm of the one who plays second.

**No. 128.** Scale of C.  In scales the fingers and thumbs do the work, the hands moving laterally only.    Quite slow.

**No. 129.** Scale of C.  Your principal difficulty, at first, will be the management of the thumb.  Observe the repeats.

**No. 131.** Scale of G.  Do not jerk nor roll the hand when the thumb passes under the fingers or the fingers over the thumb.

**No. 135.** Scale of D.  Slow at first—Moderate at last—distinct and graceful always.

**No. 139.** Scale of A.  Sometimes piano, sometimes mezzo, and sometimes forte.

**No. 142.** Scale of E.  Sometimes equal, sometimes crescendo, and sometimes diminuendo.

**No. 145.** Scale of B.  Sometimes legato, sometimes marcato, and sometimes staccato.

**No. 148.** Scale of F sharp. Apply previous remarks to all the scales. The right thumb here will need attention.

**No. 150.** Scale of G flat. Is the difference between this and No. 148 perceived by the ear or the eye? Fingered the same as No. 148.

**No. 152.** Scale of D flat. Acquire good habits in the management of the thumb.

**No. 155.** Scale of A flat. When you are sure these are right, keep the eyes on the notes as much as possible.

**No. 158.** Scale of E flat. The thumb should be passing under while the fingers are playing, in order to be in time.

**No. 162.** Scale of B flat. The fingers should pass over the thumb as it strikes. Vary the style, *p. m. f.*, ⎯⎯, ⎯⎯, ·, ⌒ and †.

**No. 166.** Scale of F. Observing the above directions, in the right amount of practice, will insure success.

**No. 172.**   Observe that the third measure in each division of these lessons is to be played four times.   See Nos. 121–5, page 53.

**No. 173.** A

**No. 174.** A

**No. 175.** A

**No. 176.** A

**No. 177.**   These exercises are to be played in three different ways.   Accent slightly the first note in each group.   Slow at first

**No. 178.**

**No. 179.**

**No. 180.**

**No. 181.** In all these exercises endeavor to strike the right key, in passing from one group to the next, without looking at your hands.

**No. 182.** Do not forget the light accent that the legato mark indicates. What is the largest interval here?

**No. 183.** Accustom yourself to various styles by practicing them here—*piano, forte, cres., dim.,* &c.

**No. 184.  THE SECOND TRIO.---(THE THREE FRIENDS' SLEIGH-RIDE—Primo.)**

Remember that the appoggiatura has no time of its own, but borrows from the note which follows it, so it will be right to commence playing each appoggiatura when you commence the count or part of the measure on which it comes. If the hand playing the upper part is small, use the thumb for the lower note in the third measure. Do you hear the sleigh-bells?

**No. 185.  THE SECOND TRIO.---(THE THREE FRIENDS' SLEIGH-RIDE—Secondo.)**

Directions for position and interlocking of arms same as on page 68. Do you hear the song of the sleigh-riders?

**No. 186.  THE SECOND TRIO.---(THE THREE FRIENDS' SLEIGH-RIDE—Terzo.)**

Give the base firmly, that there may be a good foundation. Do you hear the clatter of the horses' feet?

**No. 187.** The Common Chord of C in its three positions.
Play every common chord of C on the piano. Name the intervals combined in this chord. Name the chord and position as you play the lesson.
Move the fore arm as illustrated in the cut. Do not leave the lesson until you can make the changes with facility.

**No. 188.** The same Lesson an octave lower. When the hand is too small to reach an octave, omit the lower note.
Chords for the right hand are sometimes written on the base staff to avoid the use of so many added lines.

**No. 189.** The common chord of G in its three positions. What interval is made by the two base notes?
Play every common chord of G on the piano, before playing this lesson. Name again the intervals. Name the positions as you play them.

**No. 190.** Tonic and Dominant. What interval from upper base to lower treble?
Say whether tonic or dominant chord as you play—which position, first, second or third. Become familiar with every interval in the combinations.

**No. 191.** The same Lesson an octave lower. What interval from lower to middle notes of right hand?
Do not strike one note of a chord after another, but all exactly together, and the right hand exactly with the left.

**No. 192.** Other positions of the Tonic and Dominant. What interval from middle to upper note of right hand?
Name the chord both by tonic and dominant and by letter—also the positions. In harmony intervals are counted upwards.

**No. 193.** Other positions of Tonic and Dominant Chords.

Observe that the tones indicated by the base notes in each measure begin at the beginning of the measure—exactly with the first chord in the right hand. A note written in the middle or last part of a measure, must have its sound at the beginning of the measure, if there is no rest or other note before it. Name chords and positions as before.

**No. 194.** The Common Chord of F—Subdominant.

Before playing this lesson, play the common chord of F in all its positions. Name the chords of tonic, dominant and subdominant as they occur, with their positions. Observe the intervals of which these chords are composed.

**No. 195.** Other Positions of Chords of Tonic, Dominant, and Subdominant.

Observe previous directions Remember that in harmony intervals are counted upwards.

**No. 196.** Other Positions.

**No. 197.** Notice that in the first position of these chords the first finger strikes the middle note, and that in the second and third positions the second finger strikes the middle notes.

**No. 198.** Name chords and positions when you first play the lesson through, and *think* what they are as you play it afterwards.

# SINGING AS AN ART.

Heretofore, in this book, you have been singing as the child talks before learning its letters, without reference to the rules of the art —except as they applied equally to the piano.  You may have received hints when some fault has been prominent, but your singing thus far has only been preparatory to the study of the voice, which we now commence.

Children, and especially young persons who are near the time when the voice changes, should be exceedingly careful not to strain their vocal organs, and some should not sing at all during this process.  All should avoid fatigue, practicing at first but a little while at a time, and no one should sing when the throat is sore.  Keep yourself as healthy as possible if you wish to sing or do any thing else well. If, however, you attend to all the things here given, and which are designed to aid you to become an intelligent and accomplished musician, the singing will not be apt to occupy too much of your time.

## No. 199.  General view of the Voice and its Use.

Sing the scale without the instrument if you can, that the difficulties which you have to overcome may the more easily be perceived, especially by yourself.  Learn well the syllables and their application, as they are great aids to pronunciation and enunciation.  Adhere to the right position of body, throat and head.  Deliver the tone freely and naturally, without obstruction from lips, tongue or teeth.  Try, just here, more to throw out the voice than to make it very musical.  Fill the lungs quietly and quickly.  Use little breath.  Let the tone be neither thin or hollow.  Get the exact vowel sounds of the syllables, and give the consonants distinctly.  Sing this scale once at least, for each of the points above mentioned.

## No. 200.  Melody formed on Chords.

Observe that you are singing the tones of the tonic, dominant and subdominant chords—arpeggios for the voice.  Name the chords of which the melody and accompaniment are composed.  Notice carefully the intervals you produce in singing, and have, as soon as possible, their sounds in your memory, that you may give them with readiness and accuracy.  Your teacher will probably here explain to you those things about the organs of the voice, that are most necessary for you to know ; or you may read a description of them among the explanations in the fore part of the book.  See that the tone is well formed and delivered.  This will depend upon the pharynx, and the opening of the mouth, together with the position of the lips, tongue, teeth, &c.  See that the intonation is exact, and that the breathing is right.  Attend also to the utterance of the words.

## No. 201.  Melody on Scale.  Passing Notes.

You observe that a melody may consist of arpeggios of chords, as in the preceding lesson, or of scale forms, as here.  You perceive that the phrases in this lesson rest on, and are accompanied by tonic, dominant and subdominant chords, though there are some tones in each phrase that do not belong to the accompanying chord.  These are called passing notes.

## No. 202.

You can probably see what chords should accompany this lesson—as you can tell what chord would be made if the notes of each measure were struck together.  The accompaniment of the preceding lesson would do, though different positions in some cases would bring the upper note of the chord nearest to the vocal part.

**No. 203.** Right Muscular Action in Breathing. Phrasing.

Remember to draw the muscles under the lungs in and up when you take breath, causing the ribs and top of the chest to expand. Retain this position firmly while singing, allowing the muscles to return most gradually to their former position. Sing a phrase in a breath, using little breath especially at the beginning of the phrases. Take the time fast enough not to exhaust the lungs, and slower as your power to sustain increases. Think while you sing, whether you are in tonic, dominant, or subdominant harmony. Use syllables or vowel sounds as your teacher directs.

**No. 204.** The Chord of the Seventh. Before playing this, play and name all the positions of the chord of the seventh of G.

Observe that there are four positions of the chord of the seventh, because there are four different tones in its composition. Name as you play.

**No. 205.** You perceive that the chord of the seventh occurs only on the dominant. You see also that it is made by adding seven—not seven in the scale, but seven in the chord—to the one, three, five and eight, which make the common chord.

## SUMMER SCENES, No. I.—The Little River.

**No. 206. Quality of Tone.**

Observe that the main object of these songs is *quality of tone*. You will see that by distending the pharynx, you can make your voice more appropriate to singing about a "tavern" than a "smiling little river." This would be a wrong quality for this song. Express naturally and pleasantly the feeling or emotion that these words would excite were the scene before you and the words really your own. The pharynx should be nearly in its usual position as when you are talking—just enough distended to permit the coming into the voice of the right feeling. Nos. 206 and 207 are *not* to be sung together—they are separate songs. Sing the one that your voice reaches most easily—your teacher will direct you which to practice. For the female voice, it should be decided carefully which tones are to be sung with the lower, and which with the medium register; probably E should be in the medium. Observe breathing and articulation. Point out where the melody in these songs is made of chords, and where of scale forms.

WITH QUIET CHEERFULNESS.

1. Smiling lit - tle riv - er, From my window seen, Gliding on so gent - ly, Thro' the meadows green,
2. May our lives be like thee, Gentle little stream, Sending all a - round us Love's ce - les - tial beam,

Cheering and re - fresh - ing All up - on thy way, Brightly glow the wa - ters At the close of day.
Cheering still and bless - ing All up - on our way, Brightest at the clo - sing Of our earthly day.

**No. 207.** This number may be sung to the words and accompaniment of the preceding song, and is designed for the higher voices.

Sol sol..... do re sol do la do sol si sol do mi re

Sol sol.... do re sol do la do sol re sol

**No. 208.** SUMMER SCENES, No. II.—The Meadow Flowers.

Apply to the singing of these songs such knowledge as you have, with regard to forming and delivering the voice, taking and managing the breath, speaking the words, as well as to the special object here, viz : quality of tone. Touch the accompaniment neatly and firmly, but not too loud, and make the whole performance appropriate and natural.

CHEERFULLY.                                                                1ST TIME.  2D TIME.

1. Nodding to the streamlet In the meadow fair, } But - ter - cups and dai - sies, Roses white and red, spread.
   Are a thousand flowers, Beau - ti - ful and rare, } Lil - ies, too, and vio - lets, Everywhere are (omit)
2. How the wild-bee lingers O'er the honeyed sweets, } Modest blossoms bow - ing To the meadow - queen, green.
   How the rain-drop sparkles, As each flower it greets ; } In their perfume la - den Home of emerald (omit)

10

**No. 209.** *To discover clearly the lower and medium registers of the female voice.*

In this lesson let the G be sung in the medium, and all the other tones in the lower register; make the difference very apparent at first by causing the voice to break as it were from the lower tones to the higher, making the former firm, and perhaps masculine, and the latter softer, rounder and more fluty. After the difference in the registers is distinctly perceived, practice these exercises (Nos. 209, 210 and 211, all of which have the same accompaniment), carrying the voice, *portamento*, from the first to the second tone in each measure, as one of the first steps towards equalising the registers. All female voices do not need this practice. Men's voices requiring it can take this same exercise an octave higher.

**No. 212.** For Female Voices.

You have often been told that the great object with regard to registers is to strengthen the medium as far down at least as D. You perceive that you can sing several tones in this part of your voice with either register, and it is possible that you have been forcing your lower register too high. The only remedy is patient and persistent practice with the medium register as far down as mentioned above. So in this lesson you only sing C in the lower register—all the rest in the medium. Do not be discouraged if at first the tones are weak, they will become stronger by proper practice. The letters L. and M. stand for Lower and Medium register. You can accompany yourself with the chord of C throughout, if you choose. (Men's voices an octave higher.)

**No. 213.** In this exercise sing first in one register, and then in the other as directed by the letters, and persist in this day after day, until you can pass easily from one register to the other, and until there is some uniformity in their strength. Accompany the E's with the Tonic chord (C), and the D's with the Dominant chord (G).

**No. 214.** Strive to make the medium tones firm. Do not aspirate them when you change from the lower register. Lose as little breath as possible. Accompany the F's with the Subdominant chord (F). In both these lessons, striking the chords only often enough to sustain the voice, will give you a better opportunity to listen to the change of register.

**No. 215.** Practice of Vowel Elements.

Give each vowel its exact sound, and see that the tones are well formed and delivered. Do not distend the pharynx, or in any way try to make the voice *emotional*, for there is here no emotion to be expressed. Simply see that the tones are given out without obstruction from lips, tongue or teeth, that the lungs are well and rightly filled, and that the breath properly used, and that the vowel sounds are pure and exact. Give the accompaniment such a form as pleases you, only do not play the chords too loud. Do not carry the lower register above E. If you can, use the medium register down to C. The vowel "ah" is usually the most difficult to get exact. The syllable "Sea," used by Mr. Bassini in his works on the voice, is excellent to aid in getting the right position of mouth and throat for this vowel. Sing two or more measures in a breath, if you can, but do not exhaust the lungs. Connect the four vowels well together.

(a as in fate, e as in meet.)

**No. 216.  Practice of Consonant Elements.**

Observe that you are to give the sounds that these letters stand for in the language, and not the names of the letters themselves.  For instance, l indicates the first of the two elements that make the word "la," which is given while the end of the tongue is held against the roof of the mouth just back of the front teeth.  The sound of which m is the sign with the mouth closed, n as in no, v as in vow, th as in thou, d as in do, b as in bow, g as in go, r as in row, which should be rolled or trilled, not much, but enough to give force and distinctness.  If you wish your utterance of words in your singing to be distinct, elegant and effective, strengthen the various muscles and organs of articulation.  This is a gradual process, and is accomplished only by regular daily practice, on the principle of improving the muscles of the fingers, or any other part of the body, by appropriate exercises judiciously persisted in.  Neither the tune nor the poetry is very interesting, but you may accompany your practice by the tonic and dominant chords (the seventh may come into the dominant), making as much variety as you please, by giving the accompaniment different rhythmic and arpeggic forms.  Try the pitch also at C above this G, and accompany with the Tonic and Subdominant.  Don't fail to make thorough work of this exercise.

**No. 217.**  See that the tones are closely linked together where the legato mark indicates a connection.  Do not carry the lower register too high.  Most voices will take F in the medium.  You observe that some of the phrases in these exercises come where you can sing the lower tone in the lower register, and the upper in the medium.  It is very important that you stop and sing such phrases several times over in your daily practice, that you may equalize as quickly as possible the tones of the two registers, and thus make your voice in that respect symmetrical.  Increase the *power* of the medium register at this point, and modify the *quality* of the lower.

**No. 218.**  In this exercise female voices should be careful to make the transition from the medium to the upper register in the right way and place.  Remember that for the upper register it is probable that the vocal cords are brought together and made to vibrate as in the lower register, with this difference, that nearly one-third of their extent is held immovable by the little muscles referred to in the fore part of the book.

**No. 219.**  Remember where the repeat marks are, to sing the upper tone in the medium register, and the lower in the lower.  Repeat each phrase so marked at least four times every time you sing the lesson.

**No. 220.**  Breathe only at rests.  Let the tones be well joined, and yet distinct.  Articulate the tones without separating them.  Avoid rigidity or stiffness in the throat and lower jaw.  Do not begin the phrases loud, and do not waste any breath.  Hold the lungs full by keeping them distended rather than by closing the throat.  Leave the organs of the throat free to do their proper work.  Strike your accompanying chord at the beginning of each measure.

**No. 221.**          GALLOPADE.---(TWELFTH DUET—Secondo.)

Name tonic, dominant and subdominant chords, and their positions.   Learn both Secondo and Primo of this and the following duets, whether you play them with another or not; for they are intended to improve your chord and scale practice.

ALLEGRETTO.

**No. 222.  Sixteenth Notes.**

You observe that the value of the sixteenth notes is the same, whether they are single or in groups.  Writing them one way or the other is merely a matter of convenience.  The chords in the left hand are not full, but perhaps you can tell where the harmony is—tonic, dominant or subdominant. Which is it in the first measure?  Second?  Third?  &c.

DANCE MOVEMENT.

**No. 223.**  You perceive that this melody, and No. 224, are made of chords, with the exception of the last phrase in each.  Such female voices as are in wrong habits with regard to registers, should be careful in all these lessons to make the change in the right place.  For example—in this lesson, most persons would sing E and all above in medium, and perhaps make the last run entire, in that register.

Do mi sol do si sol fa   re do mi sol mi re        do  mi sol do do  fa  la do  si sol fa re  do        sol la si la sol fa mi re do.

**No. 224.**  This line may be accompanied by the previous accompaniment.  Learn No. 225 (page 100) in its order.

Mi sol do mi re  si  sol fa, &c.

**No. 226.**　　　　　　**GALLOPADE.**---(TWELFTH DUET—Primo.)

Observe that the two hands are playing the same melody an octave apart.　Strike the notes exactly together, and try to notice whether the accompanying harmony is tonic, dominant, or subdominant.

**No. 227.**　　　　　**SUMMER SCENES, No. III.---The Forest.**

It must be an unusually mellow lower register that can sing this first line. It will be better in the medium. Although this is marked "cheerfully," and you are, as in all these songs, to keep the midway quality of tone—the pharynx being neither distended so as to make the hollow or sombre quality, nor contracted for the bright or more gay—still there is some variation in it, which will best be attained by allowing the imagination to place you in the scenes you describe, and then give them true and natural expression. It is pleasant to be in the forest on a summer's day.

CHEERFULLY.

1.　Here!　　Here in the for - est,　Un - der the lof - ty trees..............　See!　See how the
2.　Here!　　Here in the for - est,　Dan - ces the sun - light down..............　'Mid!　'Mid the green

branch - es　Sway,　sway in the breeze..........　List!　list to the mur - mur,　Gen - tly it
leaf - lets　Swift,　swift to the ground..........　Bright!　bright is its glim - mer,　Flash - ing each

swells　a - long...........　Glad!　glad is the sum - mer,　Sweet,　sweet is her song.............
gold - en ray...........　O!　glad is the for - est　This　fair summer day..............

**No. 228.** In your accompaniments you can choose such positions of the chords as will best sustain your voice. If your ear is not yet cultivated so that it is true, take those positions which make the upper note of the chord coincide exactly with your voice. This refers more especially to the higher notes of the melody. The dash signifies that the chord is continued. The rythmic form of accompaniment adopted in No. 227, is perhaps best for these exercises. Do not practice the lessons that are too high, or too low for you. Avoid carefully all straining of the voice, especially for high tones. Remember that these lessons are principally for delivery of the voice, articulation, phrasing and the proper use of the registers.

**No. 229.** Remember that the word "seventh" means the chord of the dominant seventh.

**No. 230.**

**No. 231.**

**No. 232.**

**No. 233. Tonic, Dominant, and Subdominant, in the key of G.**
Observe that what was dominant in C is now tonic; and what was tonic in C is now subdominant; and that the chord of D is the dominant.

**No. 234.** Before playing this lesson, play the chord of the seventh of D, in all its positions. You observe that the chord of the seventh near the close of the piece has no fifth in it. It is often so used. What tone is seven in the chord of D? What is five? Three? One?

**No. 235.** Melody on Chords.

Play the accompaniment first, naming the chords, and think while you sing whether you are in tonic, dominant or subdominant harmony. Become familiar with the application of the syllables in this key. Think of intervals, in chords and in melody, as far as possible.

Do mi do sol do     la do la sol do mi fa re si do

**No. 236.** Melody of Scale Forms.

Do     Do     Fa     Fa     Sol

**No. 237.** Management of the Breath.

If your teacher has directed you to make use of any particular vowel or word, for this lesson, do not forget it. Breathe only at the rests.

Do     re     do sol do     mi     fa     mi do mi     re     mi

re     sol     re     re     mi     re sol re     do     re     do..............

**No. 238.**

Do sol do mi sol     sol fa re si do     la do fa sol la sol mi do     la do fa sol la     sol mi do     do re mi fa mi re do si la     sol la si do re mi fa sol do.
Ton.     ——     Seventh.     Ton.     Subd.     Ton.     Subd.     Ton.     ——     Subd.     Seventh.     Tonic.

**No. 239.**      QUICKSTEP.---(THIRTEENTH DUET—Secondo.)

Say whether tonic, dominant, or subdominant—common chord, or chord of the seventh; and tell their positions.

**No. 240.** Changing Position of Hands.

Adhere carefully to the fingering.

**No. 241.**      SUMMER SCENES, No. IV.---The Smiling Land.

Remember the principal object of these songs. Do not let the throat and mouth be so distended as to make a hollow sound, nor, on the other hand, so contracted as to prevent the freedom and naturalness of the tone. Above all, avoid a characterless, unmeaning tone. Take breath so as not to interfere with the sense and connection of the words. Name the chords from which the accompaniment is made.

1. O'er   the fair   and smil - ing land, The rays   of sun - light fall,     From    the fra - grant mead - ows wide   Sweet
2. Join   our voi - ces in   the strain, So cheer - ful sweet   and clear,     Sum - mer with   her hap - py birds and

per - fumes come   to all,      From   the dis - tant for - est too   The hap - py Song   birds call..............
bloom - ing flow'rs   is here,      Sing,   for 'tis   the hap - piest time   Of all   the hap - py year..............

**No. 243.**      **QUICKSTEP.---(THIRTEENTH DUET—Primo.)**

When this is well learned the movement should be pretty fast. See that there is no jerking of the hand when the thumb goes under.

**No. 244. Common Chord of Tonic, Dominant and Subdominant, in the key of D.**

First play the common chord of A (A, C♯, E, A,) in its various places upon the piano. The chord of A is the only new chord here, though the others have changed their names—that which was tonic in G now being subdominant, &c. Name chords and positions as usual.

**No. 245.**   Before playing this, play the chord of the seventh in all its positions.

**No. 246.**   Position, breathing (and phrasing), intonation, pronunciation, and delivery of the voice.

First time..............     Second time...........

Do re mi fa sol la   sol do si la sol fa mi re   mi    fa sol la si do la   sol mi sol fa mi re do re   mi    sol fa mi re do si   do

**No. 247.**                    **WALTZ.**---(FOURTEENTH DUET—Seconpo.)

Three or five is often omitted in the chord of the seventh.

**No. 248. Melody on Chords.**

Sing both melodies if the voice will reach the tones easily; if not, only one.  The same accompaniment will do for both.

Do  mi  sol  mi  do  mi  sol   fa  la  do  la  fa  la  do   sol  si  re  si  sol  si  re   do  sol  mi  sol  do

**No. 249. Management of the Breath.**

Play this accompaniment, naming the arpeggio chords and positions before singing.  Use little breath, especially at the beginning of the phrases,
when the lungs are full.  Let the tone be natural and well delivered.

Do      mi      re      sol      re      sol      mi      do      do

La      do      sol      sol      mi      sol      re      sol      re      do............

**No. 250.** Sing syllables.  Attend to delivery of voice, breathing and articulation.  Male voices carry up the chest voice as high as is pleasant.

**No. 252.**　　　　　　WALTZ.---(FOURTEENTH DUET—Primo.)

**No. 253.**　　　　　SUMMER SCENES, No. V.—The Woodland.

The upper part here is only for higher male voices—they needing the practice in upper tones—while with female voices the medium register is the one that requires most attention.  Tenors should use the falsetto above E, and make the high chest tones as pure and sweet as possible.  Name chords, and keep in mind the harmony while you sing.

1.  Hear ye the song of the wood - land!　Sweet, sweet and clear......　Gai - ly the wild birds are sing - ing,
2.  Come let us roam thro' the wood - land!　'Mid scenes so dear......　List to the voi - ces a - round us,

Sum-mer, glad sum-mer is here............　Cheer-ful - ly join in the cho - rus,　Summer, glad summer is here.
Sum-mer, glad sum-mer is here............　Yes, we will join in the cho - rus,　Summer, glad summer is here.

**No. 254.  Chords in the key of A.**
Play first the common chord of E, (E, G♯, B and E,) in its various positions.   Observe what the new chord is, and how the names and relations of the other chords have changed.   Name tonic, dominant, and subdominant, as heretofore.

**No. 255.**

REDOWA.---(FIFTEENTH DUET—Secondo.)
**No. 256.  Dotted Eighth Notes.**

**No. 257.**

Do mi sol do la do   si sol fa re mi do sol   do mi sol do la do   si sol fa re do   sol la si la sol fa mi re do.

**No. 258.** Fill the lungs well. Commence softly, with a clear tone and little breath. Retain the muscles firmly in the right position. Sing a phrase in a breath. Give as good an expression to the melody as you can. Sing both melodies or one according to your compass.

Do   mi   re   sol   re   sol   mi   do   do   fa

Do   mi   sol   do   si   sol   sol   si   re   si   do   do   fa   la   do

mi   do   do   fa   mi   do   sol   si   do..............

sol   mi   fa   la   do   la   sol   mi   mi   do   sol   do..............

**No. 260.** REDOWA.---(FIFTEENTH DUET—Primo.)

When you come to a hard spot in your lesson, practice that separately until you have overcome the difficulty, then play it in connection with the rest of the lesson.

**No. 261.** Play, name and sing, as previously directed. Keep intervals in mind.

Ton.   —   Subd.   —   Dom.   —   Ton.   Dom.   Ton.   Seventh.   Ton.

**No. 262.** Melodies of Scale Forms.

Sing both melodies if you can reach them easily; if not, only one.  Do not allow a wrong habit.

Do re mi re do si la sol la do   si do re mi fa sol fa mi re   do re mi re do si la sol la do   si do re mi fa mi fa re do.

Do si do si la sol fa mi fa la   sol la si do re mi re do si   do si do si la sol fa mi fa la   sol la si do re do re si do.

**No. 263.**　　　　SUMMER SCENES, No. VI.---The Hillside.

Choice Notes.  The tone, face and manner of the singer should express interest in the subject of the song, and should be appropriate to it.

1. To the rock-y hill-side let us go, Ere twi-light shad-ows fall, And we'll list the ech-oes as they wake At
2. On the rock-y hill-side fra-grant grows The hon-ey-suck-le sweet, And the spreading fern its o-dor sends From

ev-ery joy-ous call. List the ech-oes, List the ech-oes, As they an-swer ev-ery joy-ous call.
many a calm re-treat. 'Mid the flow-ers, And the ech-oes, Let us seek the cool and calm re-treat.

**No. 264.** Tonic, Dominant and Subdominant, in the key of E.  Dotted Quarter Note.

Before playing this, play the chord of B (B, D♯, F♯ and B,) in all its positions.  Name chords and positions in the lesson as you play them.

**No. 265.** When there are choice notes, sing either upper or lower as you can ; or each in turn, if you have compass enough.

Do mi sol mi do mi sol

**No. 266.** Dispersed Harmony.

In the dispersed chords, name the tones that are in the left hand, and those that are in the right. Name chords and positions also.

**No. 267.** Give all these exercises such expression as will make them sound best, besides attending to the more especial objects for which they are intended.

**No. 268.** Immediately after filling the lungs full you will be inclined to sing loud, and use a good deal of breath. Do neither—but make a clear, firm, yet soft tone, and increase a little towards the middle of the phrase. Make the change of register as neatly as possible.

**No. 270.**    **SUMMER SCENES, No. VII.---The Leafy Dell.**

You perceive that the harmony of the tonic is always the common chord, and so of the subdominant; but the harmony of the dominant may be the chord of the seventh. The upper part is intended for the practice of the higher voices, especially of tenors in the upper register.

1. I know a fai - ry bow - er with - in the leaf - y dell, Where 'mid the woodbine arch - es the mer - ry songbirds dwell. 'Tis
2. The wild rose blushes sweet - ly, and lifts her perfum'd head When morning wakes from slum-ber, and hours of night are fled. The

sweet to hear their mu - sic, se - cure from summer's heat, And pass the noon-tide hours... with - in their cool re - treat. O
sun-shine tries how vain - ly, to peep a - mid the leaves, With - in these woodbine arch - es that Na-ture bright-ly weaves. O

come then to the bow - er with - in the leaf - y dell, Where 'mid the woodbine arch - es the mer - ry song birds dwell.
come then to the bow - er with - in the syl - van dell, Where Nature's robes are bright - est and mer - ry song birds dwell.

**No. 271.** Tonic, Dominant and Subdominant Chords in the key of B.

Before playing and naming the chords of this lesson, practice the common chord of F sharp (F#, A#, C# and F#.) in all its positions. Can you tell readily tonic, dominant and subdominant by the sound?

**No. 273.** Tonic, Dominant and Subdominant Chords in the key of F sharp.
Before playing this, play the chord of C sharp (C♯, E♯, G♯ and C♯,) in all its positions. In what measures does the chord of tne seventh occur?

**No. 275.** Chords in G flat. Enharmonic change from F sharp.
Observe that the lesson is only to the eye different from No. 273. The numbers not found here are on pp. 100 and 101.

**No. 277.** Tonic, Dominant and Subdominant Chords in the key of D flat.
Play the common chord of A flat, (A♭, C, E♭, and A♭,) before practicing this lesson. Observe previous directions about naming chords, &c.

**No. 279.** Tonic, Dominant, and Subdominant Chords in the key of A flat.
Practice the new chord first. Observe the different names of these chords as they occur in different keys. Name them as before.

**No. 280.** Triplets.
In playing full chords having three notes for one hand, use generally those fingers which are most convenient; preferring not to use the thumb on black keys when you can easily avoid it. Using the thumb on black keys is avoided in playing scale passages, but not in playing chords.

**No. 281.**                    GALLOP.---(SIXTEENTH DUET—Secondo.)

Observe that the tonic, dominant and subdominant chords here occupy the same places upon the staff that they do in the key of A, (three sharps) but that they are a half step lower.

**No. 282.** So far as appearance is concerned the syllables apply as in the key of A.  Can you accompany this with the right chords without further direction?

**No. 283.** Take the movement slow, so that you shall exercise your power of sustaining tones, but do not exhaust the lungs.  Be careful to use little breath, especially at the beginning of the phrases.  You cannot be successful without properly controlling the abdominal muscles.

**No. 284.** Do not sing those lessons which are too high for your voice: there should be no straining to reach the upper tones.  Try various forms of accompaniment—as striking with both hands at the same time, and one after the other, &c.

**No. 286.**  **GALLOP.---(SIXTEENTH DUET—Primo.)**

This piece should sound bright and lively. To produce this effect it must be perfect—not a wrong note, not a wrong accent, not a wrong position or movement.

♩=132 8va.......

**No. 287.**  **SUMMER SCENES, No. VIII.---The Orchard.**

Still the quality of cheerfulness in the tone. Let your appearance and manner be such as one would naturally assume in uttering, with interest, words of this kind.

1. Oh the trees a - gain are all in blos - som, And the air is full of o - dors sweet And the
2. In the wood - land wilds, and in the mead - ow, See the flow - rets spring-ing fresh and fair. O the

rob - in sing - ing on the topmost bough The ear - ly sum - mer morn doth greet. Hear the rob - in !
wild bees humming at their dai - ly toil, Make mu - sic, mer - ry mu - sic there. O the wild - bees !

Hear the rob - in ! Hear the rob - in sing - ing on the top - most bough, The ear - ly sum - mer morn - ing greet.
O the wild-bees ! O the wild - bees hum - ming at their dai - ly toil, Make mu - sic, mer - ry mu - sic there.

**No. 288.**  Tonic, Dominant and Subdominant Chords in the key of E flat.
Practice the new chord first.  Give the right motion to the hand.  Observe previous directions.

**No. 289.**  ♩=100.  You observe that you never find the chord of the seventh in the tonic or subdominant.

**No. 290.**  ♩=132          QUICKSTEP.---(SEVENTEENTH DUET—Second.)
Name chords and positions.  Endeavor all the time to notice the harmony in which you are playing, whether tonic, dominant or subdominant—
common chord, or chord of the seventh.  No. 291 next, on page 101.

**No. 292.**  ♩=88          SUMMER SCENES, No. IX.---The Silver Lake.
Practice this accompaniment before singing the song.  Do not leave a chord down beyond its time.  See that the quality of tone is right.

1. Come with me, the moon is beam - ing O'er the sil - ver wa - ters of the lake so fair;
2. O de - lay not, time is fly - ing. And our com - rades call us from the peb - bly strand.

See ye not the white sail gleam - ing And the rip - ples laugh - ing in the sum - mer air? Come with me, the
E'en the gen - tle breeze is sigh - ing, As it waits to bear us from the dew - y land; 'Mid the hills in

boat is wait - ing, And the dis - tant voi - ces sweet - est mu - sic make; Come, O come, the moon is beam - ing O'er the
beau - ty gleam - ing, Still the dis - tant voi - ces sweet - est ech - oes wake; Come, O come, the moon is beam - ing O'er the

laugh - ing wa - ters of the sil - ver lake.
laugh - ing wa - ters of the sil - ver lake.

No. 293.    QUICKSTEP.---(SEVENTEENTH DUET—Primo.)

Can you distinguish the tonic, dominant and subdominant chords, in the second, by the sound, while you are playing the first?

$\cap$=132    8va.......

**No. 294.** Practice this accompaniment before singing the lesson. Notice what chords these arpeggios are made of. Notice also their positions. Are you improving in the management of your breath?

Do   mi   fa   la   sol   si   do   do   do

Do   mi   do   sol   la   do   fa   re   si   re   fa   mi............   fa   la

fa   la   do   sol   do   fa   la   do   sol   sol   si   do.

do   fa   mi   do   mi   fa   la   do   fa   mi   do   mi   si   re   fa   re   mi.

**No. 295.** Observe the directions that may be given you with regard to vowel sounds.

Do    re    do    sol

Do    si    fa    mi    re

**No. 296.** Tonic, Dominant and Subdominant Chords in the key of B flat.

Observe that the new chord here (F) was subdominant in the key of C. Play and name the chords, according to previous directions.

**No. 297.**  Pianissimo, Fortissimo, and their Abbreviations.
This you perceive is a regular march movement.  Let the time be kept with great steadiness.    Not fast.

**No. 298.**  It is believed that you can perceive the chords of which this lesson is composed without direction from the book—perhaps without aid from your teacher.  Do you know in what key you are practicing here?

Do mi sol mi mi sol do sol sol do mi do sol  do  do si  la fa la sol mi sol la  do fa la sol do mi sol  sol si re fa mi re  do  mi  sol

sol si re fa mi re  do  do mi sol mi mi sol do sol  do mi do sol  do sol sol si re fa  re si  sol si re fa re si sol si re fa mi re  do.

**No. 299.**  It will be a good plan for female voices to carry the medium register down to D, and perhaps to C.

**No. 300.**  Sing with syllables, and also with vowel sounds.

**No. 301.**      SOUVENIR.---(EIGHTEENTH DUET—Secondo.)

Endeavor to become familiar with the position of notes on added lines and spaces.

**No. 302.**    Begin each phrase with the lungs full, but with little breath: swell towards the middle of the phrase, and diminish towards the close.

**No. 304.**    With syllables and vowel sounds—delivering the tones freely, and managing the breath according to directions.

**No. 305.** SOUVENIR.---(EIGHTEENTH DUET—PRIMO.)
Make the melody as legato as possible.

**No. 306.** SUMMER SCENES, No. X.—The Vale.
You observe that the emotion to be expressed, in all these songs, is nearly the same. The pupil should be able to give this quality exactly.

1. { O'er all the smil - ing vale be - low......... Soft - ly the sum - mer shad - ows stray
{ Tint - ing with deep - er fair - er green, Mead - ow and field up - on their way.
2. { O'er all the smil - ing vale be - low Soft - ly the sum - mer bree - zes play,
{ Rip - pling the fields of shin - ing grain As o'er their feath - ery tops they stray.

Down in the vale. Down in the vale. Smil - ing in sum - mer beau - ty rare.
Down in the vale. Down in the vale. Smil - ing in sum - mer beau - ty rare.

Sweet 'tis to rove, come let us go And watch the sum - mer shad - ows there.
Sweet 'tis to rove, come let us go And watch the rip - pling corn - leaves there.

13

**No. 307.**  Tonic, Dominant, and Subdominant Harmonies in the key of F.

It is hoped that your reviewing has been so perfect that you can turn back and play any lesson perfectly.  Try it.

**No. 308.**  You will observe that there are no chords in this lesson that you have not practiced before.

**No. 309.**  Remember that an important object of this method is, to make you *understand* as well as *execute*, both in singing and accompanying.

Do  mi  sol  do  si  re      si  re  sol  si    do  mi      do  mi  sol  do  la  fa    re    sol  si    do

Do  sol  do  mi  sol  si    sol  si  re  sol    mi  do      do  sol  do  mi  fa  la    si  sol  si  re  sol    do

**No. 310.**            AU SUISSE.---(NINETEENTH DUET—Secondo.)

You will observe that the accent here is different from previous lessons in which there were six eighth notes in the measure.

**No. 312.**            **SUMMER SCENES, No. XI.—The Brooklet.**

Right quality of tone—clear and distinct articulation—right breathing and management of the breath, &c.

1. By the brook-let clear where the wil-low boughs sway, In the soft wind from the west, Is the grass-y slope and the
2. Yes the brook-let sings where the wil-low bends low, And my heart joins in the song, And the hap-py flow'rs on the

flow-ers so gay Of the home I love the best; O the soft wind from the pine hills comes with
grass-y slope glow, And I join their bright-eyed throng; Then the soft wind comes with per-fumed breath from

per-fume on its wings, And the wil-low waves and the flow-ers look up, And the brook-let gai-ly sings.
off the wes-tern hills, And it fans my cheek and it kiss-es the flow'rs, And the wil-low branch-es fills.

**No. 313.**            **AU SUISSE.---(NINETEENTH DUET—Primo.)**

You will find that different expressions may be given to this duet. Try several—and agree with your companion upon the one that you like best.

**No. 314.**  Observe that the thumbs are held on D while the fingers move over them.  Play the third measure in each section four times.

**No. 315.**  In both these exercises keep the hands in as good position and as still as possible.

**No. 225.**  Scale and Arpeggio in C.

**No. 242.**  Scale and Arpeggio in G.

**No. 251.**  Scale and Arpeggio in D.

**No. 259.**  Scale and Arpeggio in A.

**No. 269.**  Scale and Arpeggio in E.

No. 272.  Scale and Arpeggio in B.

No. 274 & 276.  Scale and Arpeggio in F sharp, and Scale and Arpeggio in G flat together.
You perceive that the keys of F♯ and G♭ differ only in their representation : to the ear they are the same.

No. 278.  Scale and Arpeggio in D flat.
There is nothing more important to your playing than these scales.  They should be practiced daily and thoroughly.  Adhere to the fingering.

No. 285.  Scale and Arpeggio in A flat.

No. 291.  Scale and Arpeggio in E flat.

No. 303.  Scale and Arpeggio in B flat.

No. 311.  Scale and Arpeggio in F.

**No. 316.** TRANSPOSITION. Here is a cadence of four chords, viz.: tonic, subdominant, dominant and tonic. These, taken in their three positions, make a musical section of eight measures. Play this section in all the keys, transposing by fifths and also by fourths. It will aid you, to think, of tonic, dominant and subdominant, and their positions, as you play. The beginning in G is given.

**No. 317.** Play this section of cadences in all the keys. It is given partly in G—enough to aid you to commence right. See that every dominant chord has a seventh in it. Transpose both by fifths and by fourths. Name the chords and their positions as you play. This is a very important exercise; do not stop practicing it until it is perfect.

**No. 318.** Observe that you tell by the base what chord you are to play, and by the treble what position of the chord. Remember that when the base note has no figure under it the common chord is indicated, and when "7," the chord of the seventh.   **No. 319.** Remember that the dash continues the effect of the previous figure.

**No. 320.** Observe that the seventh is always a step below the eighth in the chord of the seventh. A 7 but a half-step below would not sound well.   **No. 321.** Notice that the chord of the seventh is always a dominant chord. Name chords and positions as you play.

**No. 322.** Were you to put the right seventh into a tonic chord it would instantly become a dominant chord, and the key would be changed.   **No. 323.** Play each lesson until it is perfectly familiar. Observe directions carefully.

**No. 324.** Do not neglect to name the chords and their positions.   **No. 325.** Name by letter, and by tonic, dominant and subdominant.

**No. 326.** The figures ⅜, or any other figure of the common chord, indicate the common chord—just what would be indicated if no figures were printed. Sometimes used to prevent mistakes.

**No. 327.** In this lesson make the change from the common chord to the chord of the seventh, in the last chord but one, with as little movement as possible.

**No. 328.** Notice that you have here two chords to one treble note.

**No. 329.** The chord of the seventh always calls for something more.

**No. 330.** To make the changes where the figures 87 occur, eighth notes must be used.

**No. 331.** You are here to play the chord with each base note, according to the group of figures—the highest figure of course indicating the position—selecting the octave in which voices will most easily sing. It is readily seen that when the treble or highest part is printed with the base, figures are needed only to indicate the chords, as the treble shows the positions: therefore one or two figures of the common chord, or the absence of them, may indicate the common chord, and simply "7" the chord of the seventh. If the chords are merely to accompany voices, it is not necessary even where a base alone is printed, to indicate the exact position of each chord, and the usual mode of few or no figures may be adopted.

**No. 332.** Chords in the left hand, arpeggio and scale forms in the right. Accent the first note of the legato groups

**No. 333.**   After practicing this lesson where it is written, transpose into the key of G. Vary the expression.

**No. 334.**   Transpose this into the key of F. The voice may join in all these lessons, with syllables or vowel sounds.

**No. 335.**   Transpose into D. Sometimes marcato.

**No. 336.**   Transpose into B flat. Cres. and dim.

**No. 337.**   Transpose into A. Piano and forte.

**No. 338.**   Transpose into E flat. · Various accents.

No. 339.

No. 340.    These exercises should be so learned that you can play them without looking at the notes.    See that the hands are quiet and graceful.

No. 341.    By the continued practice of these exercises you will acquire a beauty and ease of execution that you can get in no other way.

No. 342.    You perceive that there is but one measure here of the descending exercise.    See if you can play the whole without the notes.

14

**No. 343.** Suspensions.

You know that a chord may have tones played or sung with it that do not belong to it, and that all such tones we have heretofore called " passing notes." Now when these "passing notes" are somewhat dwelt upon and accented, they form what are called " *Suspensions;*" probably because they suspend, as it were, for an instant the effect of the true chord. This *suspense* is enjoyed by musical people after they have made a certain degree of attainment. Play the base alone first—naming the chords—then tell which tone of the first chord is suspended or delayed—and by what? Then the next, and so on all through.

**No. 344.** Chromatic Scale. Diatonic Scale. Accidentals.

After learning to play this scale correctly, sing it with vowel sounds as well as syllables. Try it also commencing with other tones than C.

Do   di   re   ri   mi   fa   fi   sol   si   la   li   si  do.       Do   si   se   la   le   sol   se   fa   mi   me   re   ra   do.

**No. 345.** You perceive that these chromatic tones must be either passing notes or suspensions, as none of them belong to tonic, dominant or subdominant chords. Point to where both chromatic and diatonic tones form the one, and where they form the other. In which suspension is the interval a half-step? In which a step? Which do you like best?

**No. 346.** Since there is but one kind of interval in the chromatic scale, there can be really but one chromatic scale—it therefore makes no difference at what pitch you begin it, or in what key you play or sing it, or with what chords you accompany it. The only difference is in the representation or notation, and sometimes in the place of accenting. You perceive that the chromatic tones here, with a single exception, are passing notes, and should be played with a certain degree of quickness to be agreeable. Name the chords that accompany.

**No. 347.** NATURAL. You observe that the second finger is mostly used to strike the black keys.

**No. 348.** Commencing on the dominant. You will find the thumb and second finger the principal actors in this performance.

**No. 349.** Play each lesson piano, mezzo, forte, crescendo and diminuendo, but not too fast.

**No. 350.** Endeavor to have the control and mastery of every note in each lesson. To do this commence slow.

**No. 351.** When you discover a passage in any key to be a part of the chromatic scale, there is no difficulty in knowing what notes to strike.

No. 352.

No. 353.

No. 354.

No. 355.

No. 356.

No. 357.

No. 358.

**No. 359.** Inversions of the Common Chord (Tonic).

Before playing this lesson, play the common chord of C, with three for the base note, instead of one, then again with five for the base.  Observe that C, E and G make the common chord of C in whatever order they are taken.  Name the inversions as you play.  Which hand do positions refer to?  Which hand or part, inversions?  How many positions has the common chord?  How many inversions?  You observe that when the base is one, the chord is not inverted.  It is then said to be *direct.*  You observe that the two inversions of the common chord may take place with either of these positions.  It is *very important* that you practice this transposition first by fifths, and then by fourths, until you can play the lesson readily, smoothly and perfectly in any key.  It is written out in G, to help you in the first step, which is usually the hardest.  If you cannot do this work, it will be because you have not taken the previous steps well, and you must go back and take them again, if you wish to be a really intelligent and appreciative performer and listener.  Remember that your mind must work as well as your fingers, if you would grow healthfully in all your musical powers.

*First Transposition.*
Your teacher and the author of this book wish to make you equally familiar with all the keys.  Will you help us?

**No. 360.** The same in Arpeggio form.
Transpose into all the keys.  Name chords and inversions as before.

*Another arpeggio form of the same lesson.*

**No. 361.** Inversions of the Common Chord (Dominant and Tonic).

Before playing this lesson, play the different positions of the chord of G, first with three (B) for the base note, then with five (D), naming both inversions and positions as you play.  While practicing the lesson, name as follows : " Common chord of C direct, common chord of G direct, common chord of G first inversion, G second inversion, G first, C direct," &c.  Accustom yourself, also, to naming the chords in this way : " Tonic direct, Dominant direct, Dominant first inversion, Dominant second," &c.  When not naming the chords, it is very important that you should acquire the habit of thinking what harmony you are in.  Do not be discouraged if at first the transposition is difficult.

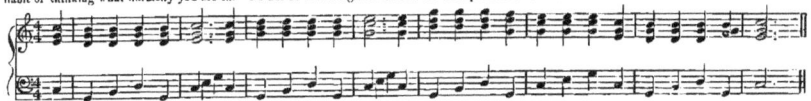

*First Transposition.*
After playing this lesson in all the keys, it will be an excellent plan to give it an arpeggio form and transpose again.

**No. 362.** Inversions of the Common Chord, (Subdominant, Dominant and Tonic.)
Before playing this lesson, play the different inversions of the common chord of F in all its positions. This will be more difficult to transpose, but should by all means be done, naming the chords as you play. Transpose into all the keys.

*First Transposition.*
Play this also in arpeggio forms, if you can. We are very desirous that you should understand as well as execute.

**No. 363.** Remember that the lowest note of a chord is its base, and by that you ascertain whether the chord is direct or inverted, and that the highest note, which is the treble, determines its position. Here, the chord is mostly in the base and played with the left hand, but that makes no difference, as the tones of a chord will produce that chord when heard together, no matter where they are, or which is highest and which lowest—only the highest determines with regard to position and the lowest to inversion. How many different tones has the common chord? Then how many different tones can be highest? (Remember that in harmony tones having the same name are not regarded as different tones. So in the common chord of C, C may be highest, making the first position, then E making the second, then G the third; but C an octave above the first would be regarded as repeating the first position.) How many different tones can be lowest? As the same number of tones can be lowest as highest, why are there *three* positions and but *two* inversions?

Play this base with the upper part of the above lesson after having learned it with the base set to it.

Then try this. You perceive that the same harmony is used in both of these bases, but that different effects are produced by breaking up the chords into arpeggio groups.

**No. 364.** Before commencing each lesson, remember that only three chords are used—tonic, dominant and subdominant.

**No. 366.** Think what they are in the key before you—it will aid you in recognising and naming the inversions.

**No. 368.** Play the scales in the order of their numbers. When the first inversion of the common chord occurs in the first, or accented part of the measure, it is common to omit the third in the other part of the chord.

**No. 370.** Remember that tonic, dominant and subdominant, are decided by that which is ONE *of the chord*, and not always by the base, which may be one three or five.

**No. 372.** After learning the lesson, you may sing with the playing.

**No. 374.** If you sing, use syllables or vowel sounds.

**No. 376.** Those only need to sing whose voices are not in tune.

**No. 378.** Singing the second part will be good practice for *tuning*.

**No. 380.** Avoid doubling the third in the common chord.

**No. 382.** One of a chord may be four or five of the SCALE.

**No. 384.**

**No. 386.**

**No. 388.**

*After these scales are learned,* in the order of their numbers, repeat each one as you practice it daily, six times at least, varying the expression each time. Observe the same plan with regard to the arpeggios. Never play so fast as to make a false note, or in any way so as to mar the neatness and elegance of the performance. It is an excellent plan to practice your stated time by the watch or clock, and never to fail in punctuality or faithfulness.

**No. 365.**

**No. 367.**

**No. 369.**

**No. 371.**

**No. 373.**

**No. 375.**

Now is the time to give the finishing corrections to any faults that may remain in your positions and movements. These scales should by all means be learned by heart, with the exact fingering belonging to each; for many important lessons follow that will take for granted this ability on your part, and that can hardly be learned satisfactorily without it. Endeavor to know one scale or key just as well as another—be at home in all.

**No. 377 & 379.**

**No. 381.**

**No. 383.**

**No. 385.**

**No. 387.**

**No. 389.**

**No. 390.** Besides observing the directions with regard to management of the breath and articulation already given, remember that the most im-

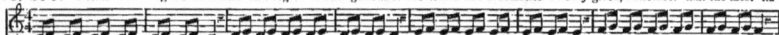

**No. 391.**

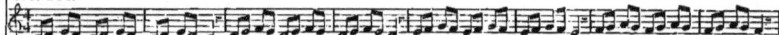

**No. 392.**

**No. 393.** ABBREVIATION.

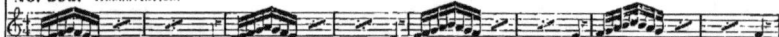

**No. 394.** If you can sing some of these lessons in two, three or four keys, it will add materially to your improvement. Use syllables in singing,

**No. 395.**

**No. 396.**

**No. 397.** Never pass a lesson because it does not please you, nor for any other cause, until it is thoroughly learned; as each one is a stepping

**No. 398**

portant thing about these exercises is their transposition and practice in those keys which will bring them within the compass of your voice.

and also practice the lessons with the vowel sound "ah."   Give each note its proper time.   Do not hurry in one place and lag in another.

stone, or stairway to the next.   If you can not sing the exercise  in this key, transpose it to another.

**No. 399.** In this lesson the right hand plays the accompaniment, and the left hand crosses over.

**No. 400.** In this lesson the left hand plays the accompaniment, and right hand plays the melody and crosses over.

**No. 401.**  Before playing this lesson, play the chord of the seventh of G direct, then with three for the base, then with five, and finally with seven; these will be inversions of the chord of the seventh.  It is very common to omit three in the right hand when you have it in the base, and so of five, and invariably so of seven.  You perceive that the chord of the seventh is not a good chord to stop on—it seems unquiet, and, as it were, wants to find a resting place.  The tonic chord will always be that resting place, and the going of the chord of the seventh to its resting place is called its resolution.  Although the chord of the seventh, either direct or inverted, generally goes to the tonic chord, the resolution is sometimes to other chords, as will be seen.  You perceive that there are *three* inversions of the chord of the seventh, and you probably see that the reason is that there are four different tones in it, while there are but three in the common chord.  You will observe that the third inversion of the chord of the seventh always resolves to the first inversion of the common chord on the tonic.  It is so important that these chords be equally familiar to you in all the keys that we ask again that you will not fail to do this work of transposition most thoroughly, naming (especially at first) every chord as you play.  It will aid you if you will play the chord of the seventh belonging to each key, in all its forms, before making the transposition.

*First Transposition.*

**No. 402.**  The same, with another position.  To be transposed into all the keys.

*First Transposition.*

**No. 403.**  The same, with other positions.  To be transposed into all the keys.

*First Transposition.*

**No. 404.**  The same, in arpeggio forms.  It will be difficult to transpose this, but if you can play it in two or three other keys it will be an excellent plan.  Try F, D, and B♭.

**No. 405.**  The same harmonies in another arpeggio form.  If you can transpose this lesson, play it also in G, A, and B♭.

**No. 406.**  Name the chords and their inversions first, and while playing do not allow one to pass without thinking what it is.

**No. 408.** How many inversions has the common chord? How many the chord of the seventh? What is the base in the third inversion? Always commence your practice so slow that you can play without hesitation or a mistake. Continue to do so, and your lessons will come to be fast enough themselves—*never hurry*. These directions apply especially to the arpeggios and other exercises for daily practice, which please to learn carefully, in the order of their numbers. You will find the exercises belonging to this page on page 120.

**No. 410.** What is the base in the second inversion? What in the first? What is the base when the chord is direct?

**No. 412.** The voice may take the upper part with the piano.      **No. 414.** This will benefit voices that need tuning.

**No. 416.** If you sing, use syllables.      **No. 418.** Try also singing the second.

**No. 420.** See if you can sing the third.      **No. 422.** Try also the base.

**No. 421.** To what inversion of the common chord does the third inversion of the seventh always resolve?
LEGATO.

**No. 426.** Each inversion you perceive has its own peculiar sound or effect. Learn to recognise it as soon as possible.

**No. 428.** It is important that you should know these chords when you hear them, as well as when you see their notation.

**No. 430.** Do you now feel that you are familiar with tonic, dominant and subdominant harmonics, in all their positions and inversions?

## No. 432. The Chord of the Ninth.

Where is the chord of the ninth always found, on tonic, dominant or subdominant? Of what tones is it composed? With what chord is it intimately connected? How do you like it? You may perhaps remember that we have really used this chord before, but have called the ninth a passing note, or a suspension. Remember that the effect of the sharp in the tenth measure continues through the next. To what key do you modulate there?

There should be such thoroughness and solidity in your progress, that you can at any time turn back and execute well any previous lesson or piece. Observe the following two things with regard to them, viz: a piece played or sung straight along, without expression, is like a marble statue, having a certain kind of beauty, but after all cold and dead; while a piece played or sung with true feeling or expression is like the beautiful form which has warmth and life. The power of feeling and expressing music is a gift bestowed in different degrees, but all may cultivate it.

Learn these arpeggios in the order of their numbers.   After all are learned, let your daily practice of them begin at the *last* one and play to the *first.*   You will perceive that the dominant seventh makes the transposition by fourths more agreeable than the other.

**No. 407.**                                          **No. 409.**

**No. 411.**                                          **No. 413.**

**No. 415.**                                          **No. 417.**

**No. 419 & 421.**                                    **No. 423.**

**No. 425.**                                          **No. 427.**

**No. 429.**                                          **No. 431.**

Play these exercises in all the keys—sometimes forte, sometimes piano, sometimes crescendo, sometimes diminuendo, sometimes legato, sometimes staccato ; but never hurriedly.

**No. 433.**   Attend carefully to such reviewing as your teacher assigns to you.

**No. 434.**   The great work of becoming a good musician must be done by yourself.   No one can learn for you.

**No. 435.**   Keep in mind the important place that technics hold in your musical education.

**No. 436.**   Let nothing prevent your practicing all the exercises on this page, in all the keys, until they are *your own*—that is, perfectly learned.

**No. 437.**

**No. 438.**

**No. 439. Accidentals used in representing a Key.**

This lesson, you perceive, is just as much in the key of G as though the sharp had been put at the beginning in the usual way. Notice that the sharp makes the line or space on which it occurs stand for a tone a half step higher than it otherwise would, but that this effect only continues through the measure. It is easily seen that changing the signification of the line or space once for all, as is done when the sharp is used as a signature, saves time and trouble.

**No. 440.** You see that sharps and flats when used as accidentals have not so much power as when used as signatures, or rather their power does not extend so far. In what key is this lesson? Name the chords.

**No. 441.** Notice that the first note in the seventh measure is F sharp, although no sharp is placed immediately before it. The effect of an accidental continues from one measure to the next, if the last note of the one and the first note of the next are on the line or space that is affected. In what key is this lesson?

**No. 442. Modulation.**

You see by this lesson that a piece of music is not necessarily kept in one key throughout, and that modulations may produce pleasant variety. You also see that for the short time we are out of the key of C, it is not worth while to change the signature, but is better to represent the key of G by accidentals. Name the chords by letter, as, "common chord of C direct, common chord of C first inversion," &c.; and also by tonic, dominant and subdominant, as, "tonic direct, tonic first inversion," &c. In the seventh measure the first and second chord are dominant in the key of C, and the third and fourth are dominant in the key of G. The only chord in the eighth measure is tonic in G, and the first and second chords in the next measure dominant in C, &c. What is tonic in G? What is dominant in C? What is subdominant in G? What is tonic in C? Observe that the accidentals here are not passing notes, but regular tones in the chords.

**No. 443.**                    The Happy Group.

You perceive that these chromatic tones are passing notes only, and do not cause modulation.   Give finish and completeness to your work.

MODERATO.

**No. 444.  Modulation by the Flat Seventh.**

You perceive that the seven here referred to, is of the scale.   What does the tonic chord in the key of C become by adding B flat to it?   In what key is it then dominant?   What other modulation takes place?   What tones are used that do not cause a modulation?   Sing syllables first.

Sad - ly  the night wind Sighs o'er the plain, But with the  morn-ing Light comes a - gain.   So when the  sad heart Moans on its way,

Ev - er re - mem - ber  Joy comes with day.   *Postlude.*

In order to give the imagination more freedom, pieces are composed for the voice, *without words*, called SOLFEGGIOS. The best singers regard the practice of solfeggios important not only for the object mentioned above, but for improvement in the management of the breath, (and consequently in phrasing,) and in execution: while the effort to express joy, gaiety, cheerfulness, courage, &c., as well as the more plaintive and sad emotions by their means, is of the greatest importance in developing the power to make use of different *qualities of tone*. As there are no words in solfeggios to give definiteness to the expression, as far as it relates to emotion and consequent quality of tone, it is obvious that such an interpretation of the music may be given as will be in accordance with its character. It will be found in all solfeggios that several interpretations can be given with almost equal propriety, and in some cases emotions quite opposite may in turn be expressed without violence to the music.

**No. 445.**      SOLFEGGIO ONE.

To what key do you modulate here? By what tone? Be very careful to notice and name the inversions that occur, and then think of them as you sing and play. Observe that it is not worth while to change the syllables to the key of G in the first modulation, because it is so short.

What key is made by the tones C, D, E, F, G, A and B ?   What key by the tones C, D, E, F♯, G, A and B ?   What key is this piece said to be in ?   What other key occurs in it ?   What is the process of going to the key of G here called ?—and what is the process of going back to the key of C called ?   Endeavor to see what chords the arpeggio groups are made of.   If you have any difficulty in doing this, condense by striking all at once.

**No. 446.**

The Village Green.

**No. 447.**  Transpose this Waltz into the keys of G, D, A, F, B♭, and E♭.   You observe that you go at once from the tonic of the key you are in to the dominant of the key to which you modulate.

First Transposition.

**No. 448.**                          SOLFEGGIO TWO.

This solfeggio may be transposed to a lower or higher key, to suit your voice, if necessary.  It would be an excellent plan to try it in some other key; D, for example.  Take breath only at the rests.  Be careful to make the musical meaning distinct and clear by right phrasing, and the whole performance effective by means of such things of style as you have practiced.  Sustain the long notes generally with the swelling and diminishing tone.

**No. 449.**                    THE HAPPY RETURN.---(Joyfulness.)

1. How bounds the heart at the sweet words of wel-come,    When from a-far we have come.............
2. Friends that have min-gled their pray'rs with ca-ress-ing,    Of-ten in days that are past,.............
3. This was the star that e-clipsed proud am-bi-tion,    This was the bright hope we kept.............

Back to the scenes of our fond-est re-mem-brance,    And to the dear ones at home.............
Cling to us now with a fond whis-per'd bless-ing,    Sweet-er than dreaming at last.............
Deep in our hearts, like a gem in a cas-ket,    Guard-ed by love while we slept.............

Oh, in our wak-ing how longed we to see them,    And in our sleep-ing how dear Were the
Oh, if this world can hold aught to re-pay us,    For all its sor-row and pain, 'Tis the
Al-ways we see on life's bois-ter-ous o-cean,    Spark-ling through bil-lows of foam Like the

*un poco ritenuto.............*

dreams........... that in beau-ty and bright-ness Brought the lov'd vis-ion so near.............
hour............... wreath'd with sun-shine and pleas-ure, Bring-ing us home once a-gain.............
pure............... fra-grant ro-ses of E-den, Pic-tures of wel-come at home.............

☞ In the preceding song, give right quality of tone, sufficient force in the enunciation of the consonant elements to give earnestness to the words, and be careful of the management of the breath. Is there an accidental there that is a passing note? Do you see, or rather hear, that the chord of the ninth is formed in three places in this song by the accompaniment and melody taken together? Could you transpose it a little higher or a little lower, if the present pitch does not suit your voice? It will be an excellent plan to try it in some other key.

**No. 450.** When a chromatic tone or accidental is dwelt upon a certain time, its own harmony must be given with it to make it sound well, and so a modulation takes place to another key. Where does such a modulation take place in this lesson? Observe that the first inversion of the chord of the seventh of D takes place in the fourth measure.

**No. 451. Tonic and Dominant Chords in the key of A Minor. Major and Minor Thirds.**

Before playing this lesson, play major and minor thirds in various parts of the piano. Be able to tell them by the ear as well as their signs by the eye. You observe that the dominant here is a major chord, made so, by introducing G sharp whenever the dominant occurs. Play the dominant chord using G instead of G sharp, and see how you like it. Name the chords and their positions, thus: " Common chord of A minor, first position ; same ; common chord of E major, second position, &c. You can sing while you play—either the upper parts or the base. Syllables apply as in the key of C, la to A, do to C, &c.

**No. 452. Tonic, Dominant and Subdominant in the key of A Minor.**

You perceive that the dominant and subdominant in the minor are reckoned from the key note, just as they are in the major. The dominant a fifth, and the subdominant a fourth. You probably perceive that the signature of this key is also the signature of C major. This is why the syllables apply the same. Is the subdominant a major or a minor chord? Which interval of the common chord decides whether it is major or minor? When the third is major, what kind of chord is it? When the third is minor, what?

**No. 453. Chord of the Seventh in the Minor.**

You perceive that the chord of the seventh may occur in the dominant of the minor as it does in the major. The thought may occur to you, " Why is not this sharp which occurs so often, put into the signature, and thus its use as an accidental be avoided ?" Excellent reasons for this will appear by and by. As G sharp here is for a good reason represented as an accidental, although really a tone of the key, the syllable is applied as to an accidental.

**No. 454. Inversions of Chords in the Minor.** (Learn No. 455 next, page 148.)

You observe that inversions occur in the minor chord as in major. The chord of the seventh being always a dominant chord, consequently always major does not differ from what you have been playing. It is observed that minor music is not liked at first by most learners, but it is equally true that it is liked more and more as progress is made in the knowledge and consequent appreciation of music.

**No. 456.** Inversions of Tonic, Dominant and Subdominant Chords in G Major.  Forzando.

Name the chords and their inversions.  Notice how the forzando and the grouping by the legato mark break up the natural accent of the measure.

**No. 457.**                        The Sunbeams of the Morning.

**No. 458.**        SOLFEGGIO THREE.

What emotion will this solfeggio best express—cheerfulness, joy, or the more somber, such as sadness, sorrow, &c.? What position and form do the pharynx and other organs of the voice take for the somber emotions? What for the brighter and more joyful? Remember that whatever be the expression, there must be a constant undulation of the voice: cres., dim., &c.

If you need to sing higher or lower than these solfeggios go, it is expected that you will transpose to meet the necessity.

**No. 459.**        THE GUARDIAN.—(Plaintiveness.)

1. Art thou watch-ing o - ver me, my Moth - er, From thy home a - mong the blest?...... Dost thou
2. Art thou watch-ing o - ver me, my Moth - er, In the cares and toils of life?...... Is it
3. Will thy watch be o - ver me, my Moth - er, When the day of life is o'er?...... Can I

guide my way - ward footsteps, Mother,   In the ways of   peace and   rest?   Is it  thy  sweet smile that sometimes
thy sweet voice with-in me, Mother,   That I  hear a - mid   the   strife?   When my self - ish   love to sin al -
put  my hand in thine, my  Mother,   When I  reach the   mys - tic   shore?   Wilt thou guide me   to the pleasant

bright - ens  All the dark  and  drear - y  road?   Is  it  thy  dear love that draws me up - ward   To that
lures  me,  And I  sink  be - neath  its  spell.   Dost thou come with heav'nly pow'r to save  me,   And the
wa - ters  In the fields  of  liv - ing  green?   Can  I  change these soil'd and tatter'd gar - ments   For those

pure  and  bright a - bode?
hosts  of  e - vil  quell?
robes  so  white and  clean?

**No. 460.**  Tonic, Dominant and Subdominant Chords in the key of E minor.

You improve in appreciation only by finishing and perfecting every thing you perform to the utmost, according to the taste and knowledge you have.

**No. 462.** Inversions of Tonic, Dominant and Subdominant Chords in D major.
Name the chords and their inversions.  If your hand is too small to reach all the notes of the most extended chords, omit the lower one.  Observe carefully the marks of expression.  Do all the previous lessons, songs and pieces, belong to you?  Have you forgotten, or thrown them away?

**No. 463.**                          The Holiday Party.

Nobody likes vanity and self-conceit.  Even vain and conceited people dislike it in others.  If you wish your musical performances to produce good results, let them be governed by modesty, obligingness and unselfishness—not the appearance of these qualities merely, but the reality of them.

After playing the Da Capo after the second section, play the third section which is in the key of G, then Da Capo to end the piece.          FINE.

**No. 464.**      SOLFEGGIO FOUR.

Remember to begin the phrases without expending much breath, and do not continue for any length of time with the same strength of tone; especially let the long tones be cres. or dim., or both.  It will be an excellent plan sometimes to make use of syllables.  Name the chords.

**No. 465.** Inversions of the Tonic, Dominant and Subdominant Chords in B Minor.

How would the syllables apply here in singing?  What is five in this scale?  What is five in this tonic chord?  What is five in the dominant? In the subdominant?  It is hoped that you understand, as well as perform correctly, everything thus far.  What kinds of thirds occur here?

**No. 467.** Inversions of Tonic, Dominant and Subdominant Chords in A major.

You observe that you have short scale forms sometimes in the base, when you have chords in the right hand. Observe which of these base notes are the proper bases of the chords, and which are passing notes.

**No. 468.**

## The Old Guard.

Remember that the difficulty of a piece is much increased when you perform it to others. Play only what you are absolutely sure of. Name chords, modulations, suspensions and passing notes.

SOTTO VOCE. ♩=92.

**No. 469.** **THE INVITATION TO THE DANCE.---(Gaiety.)**

In this piece the principal melody is for the instrument, and the piece will consequently tax your power of doing two things at once. Make the fingers and voice independent of each other as far as may be necessary. If sung by a male voice, the upper part should be taken.

O come, love, with me Where the soft sun-beams glance, And join the gay group In the song and the

dance— Each move-ment of grace Brings de-light to the eye, Each strain of the song Is a true pleasure

nigh. { A - way then with sor - row, Bid cares all de - part. Bring nev - er a shad - ow Up - on the young
{ In each thought and ac - tion Let true friendship guide, That e'en in our glad - ness Good will may pre-

heart, } O come then with me Where the soft sunbeams glance, And join the gay group In the song and the dance.
side. }

**No. 470.** Inversions of Tonic, Dominant and Subdominant Chords in F♯ minor.

**No. 472.** Inversions of Tonic, Dominant and Subdominant Chords in E major.

Keep faithfully, for the present, to the habit of naming chords and inversions, passing notes, suspensions, &c.

ADAGIO.

**No. 473.** The Willow by the River.

Remember that $f$ here does not indicate so great a degree of strength as it would in a maestoso movement.

ANDANTE CON GRAZIA.

**No. 474.**                    SOLFEGGIO FIVE.

Be careful in all these solfeggios to produce such a quality of tone, and consequently to give such an emotional expression, as the structure of the music will properly admit.   Be careful also to make the musical meaning distinct and clear by right phrasing, and the whole performance effective by the right use of the various things of style and expression.   Do you think what the harmony is as you play and sing?

**No. 475.** Inversions of Tonic, Dominant and Subdominant Chords in C♯ Minor.

18

**No. 477.** Inversions of Tonic, Dominant and Subdominant chords in B major.

**No. 478.** Be as careful in these keys to name and recognise the chords, as in the more common ones.

**No. 479.** Inversions of Tonic, Dominant and Subdominant Chords in G♯ minor.
Observe that the *double sharp* is similar to the character indicating the thumb.   Do not mistake one for the other.

**No. 481.** Inversions of Tonic, Dominant and Subdominant Chords in F♯ major.

**No. 482.** In what other key would a change of signature bring this lesson, without changing the notes on the staff?   Play it in that key.

**No. 483.** Inversions of Tonic, Dominant and Subdominant Chords in D♯ minor.

**No. 485.** Inversions of Tonic, Dominant and Subdominant Chords in G♭ Major.

**No. 486.** Can you tell as readily whether you are in tonic, dominant or subdominant harmony, as when playing in the more usual keys?

**No. 487.** Inversions of Tonic, Dominant and Subdominant Chords in E♭ minor.

**No. 489.** Inversions of Tonic, Dominant and Subdominant Chords in D♭ major.

**No. 490.** Try to become familiar with the peculiarity of each inversion. Do not neglect to name the chords.

**No. 491.** Inversions of Tonic, Dominant and Subdominant Chords in B♭ minor.

**No. 493.**  Inversions of Tonic, Dominant and Subdominant chords in A♭ major.

Observe that the time of this is slow.  Name the chords.  Give the ending as marked.  Where do passing notes commence in the base?

ADAGIO.

**No. 494.**                  Moonlight on the rippling Water.

If  G flat were added to this signature, what major key would be indicated?  Would putting a flat before every G produce the same effect?  Then what key is the third section of this piece in?  It must be a very simple piece of music that will not give pleasure if well performed.  In playing for your friends you will do well to be governed by this principle.  Committing to memory such pieces as you can best perform is an excellent plan.

**No. 495.**                    **ADALIDA.—(Sorrow.)**

Do not exaggerate those movements of the body which properly accompany the expression of emotion,—on the other hand do not cramp yourself with too much restraint,—naturalness and freedom are essential to an effective musical performance.

CON ESPRESSIONE.

D. C. 1. 'Neath the wil - low she is sleep - ing, And the flow - ers bloom the new mound o'er,   Ad - a - li - da!   Ad - a -
2. 'Neath the wil - low she is sleep - ing, And my wea - ry heart is lone and sad,   Ad - a - li - da!   Ad - a -
3. 'Neath the wil - low she is sleep - ing, But I'll wake my life - work to ful - fil,   Ad - a - li - da!   Ad - a -

FINE.

- li - da!   We shall see thy form on earth no more.   Oh! her voice made sweet - est mu - sic,   As its
- li - da!   What is left on earth to wake me glad.   Oh! her foot - steps in my path - way,   Made the
- li - da!   Can thy spir - it guard and guide me still?   Is thy home now with the an - gels,   Are they

ad lib. D. C. to first verse.

mel - low cadence rose and fell;   And her eye beamed joy and brightness, On the faithful heart she loved so well. Ah......
dark - est windings gleam with light;   And her pure love with me ev - er Gave new strength to keep more near the right. Ah......
far a - way from us or near?   Do they help us in our strug - gles With the e - vils that be - set us here? Ah......

* These triplets will hardly be sung in exact time because of the difficulty of making a group of three go with a group of two.  They may be made something like the corresponding groups in the prelude.

**No. 496.**  Inversions of Tonic, Dominant and Subdominant chords in F minor.

Observe that this is very slow.  Give expression as marked, especially the forzando.

ADAGIO.

**No. 498.**  Inversions of Tonic, Dominant and Subdominant Chords in E♭ major.
Do not take the time too fast.   Remember that maestoso includes a rather marcato style of performance in the fortissimo passages.

MAESTOSO.

**No. 499.**                    The Swallows' flight over the Camp.
LEGGIERO.

1st time.        8va...............loco.   2d time...........................

Learn these pieces and songs so thoroughly that you can play them at any time, and in any place.   If you can perform them without the notes, so much the better.   When asked to play for others, do not hesitate and wait to be coaxed, but pleasantly and promptly comply.   Select a piece that you are *sure of*, even if it be one of your older and simpler lessons; for they, if *well performed*, will be pleasing—while the most beautiful piece, if bungled, is only listened to out of politeness, and is painful rather than agreeable.  Many injudicious persons will perhaps praise you when you have played for them, and will even do so when you have played very poorly.  Do not be misled by such praise, but have a higher motive than a desire for it.

**No. 500.**                          **SOLFEGGIO SIX.**

You perceive that this solfeggio is best adapted to express boldness or courage.  Let the quality of tone correspond to this emotion.  It will be a good plan to sing it a part of the time with syllables.  If it does not accommodate the pitch of your voice, can you transpose it?

MODERATO.

**No. 501.** Inversions of Tonic, Dominant and Subdominant Chords in C minor.

Apply syllables as if the tones were in Eb major.  Sing the second part.  Try also the third—and the base.

**No. 503.** Inversions of Tonic, Dominant and Subdominant chords in B♭ major.

In passing from the sixth to the seventh measure, let the thumb of the right hand slide from the black to the white key without being raised. Remember that *andantino* includes a graceful effect. The second section of this piece is a little bolder, still it should all be played *legato*.

ANDANTINO.

**No. 504.**          The Butterfly among the Flowers.

You see that instead of modulating by the sharp fourth in this lesson, we go back to the key of E flat for one change, and to save the trouble of writing so many accidentals, the signature of this key is used. Although the time is as here indicated by the metronomic mark, the piece may be a *little* faster if it can be played with ease and elegance. Supply the marks of expression according to your own taste.

♩=132. THIRTY-SECOND NOTES.

No. 505.    THE DYING SOLDIER.—(Anguish and Joy.)

AGITATO.

1. The fear - ful night is clos - ing round me, On the blood - y field I lie; Is this
2. What light is this so strange - ly gleam - ing? Ah! I see the dear old home; Hark! I
3. A - gain that light so strange is gleam - ing; Ah! 'tis far more glo - rious now, And its

death now creep-ing o'er me; Must I here for - got - ten die? Fa - ther! Moth - er! O, the
hear fam - il - iar voi - ces; And they say, "Come, sol - dier, come." Fa - ther! Moth - er! O, the
rays of daz-zling white - ness Seem to rest up - on my brow— Fa - ther! Moth - er! I am

an - guish of this dread - ful hour to tell; But a - las, no help can reach me, Dear ones,
sweet - ness of your kind and ten - der care; But a - las, the vi - sion's van - ished, And I'm
hap - py, for the an - gels round me stand, And I know that they will bear me Up - ward

all, a long fare - well.
go - ing, but not there.
to that bet - ter land.

No. 506. Inversion of Tonic, Dominant and Subdominant Chords in G Minor.

19

**No. 508.** Inversions of Tonic, Dominant and Subdominant Chords in F major.

Name chords and inversions as before. Think of the harmony as you play. Adhere to right positions and movements.

**No. 509.**         Proudly floats the Banner.

Name the chords and the inversions. Think of the harmony while you play. Give the right expression and learn perfectly.

**No. 510.**   SOLFEGGIO SEVEN.

This solfeggio is too high for most voices, and to be useful *must* often be transposed. If the arpeggios in the right hand are too low when transposed, there will be no objection to playing them in different positions. Is your voice becoming purer, more uniform and symmetrical? Are you improving in regard to blending registers, sustaining tones, and economising the breath? Are your pronunciation and enunciation good, and your execution neat and distinct? And last, but not least, can you give the quality of tone corresponding to the emotion that you wish to express?

CANTABILE.

Ah............   Ah............

FINE.

Ah............   Ah............

D. C.

Ah............   Ah............   Ah............

**No. 511.** Inversions of Tonic, Dominant and Subdominant Chords in D minor.

**No. 455.** Scale and Arpeggio in A minor.

What kind of minor scale is represented first? What next? What kind of common chord does the arpeggio make?

**No. 461.** Scale and Arpeggio in E minor.

It is very important that you should become familiar with minor scales and chords in all the keys.

**No. 466.** Scale and Arpeggio in B Minor.

Learn these scales perfectly in the order of their numbers, then practice them daily until you can play them without notes.

**No. 471.** Scale and Arpeggio in F♯ minor.

No one can be regarded as having made high attainments in music, who does not know the minor keys nearly as well at least as the major.

**No. 476.** Scale and Arpeggio in C♯ minor.

It is observed that the longer we study music, and the better we know it, the more we like the minor with its chords, scales and pieces.

**No. 480.** Scale and Arpeggio in G♯ minor.

Observe that F double sharp is the same tone on the piano as G. Do not confound the character indicating it with the thumb mark.

**No. 484 & 488.** Scale and Arpeggio in D♯ and E♭ minor.

The minor scales from the signature four sharps to the signature four flats, although not so common as the others, should be thoroughly learned.

**No. 492.** Scale and Arpeggio in B♭ minor.

Let us remind you of the importance of learning these scales by heart. Which is harmonic, and which is melodic?

**No. 497.** Scale and Arpeggio in F minor

These like the major scales should have variety of expression, sometimes *p*, sometimes *f*, sometimes *cres.*, and sometimes *dim.*

**No. 502.** Scale and Arpeggio in C minor.

It will be an excellent plan sometimes to join with your voice in such of these scales as are within your compass.

**No. 507.** Scale and Arpeggio in G minor.

It is hoped that you will not find the practice of these minor scales so difficult as to tire you of them before they are learned.

**No. 512.** Scale and Arpeggio in D minor.

Cultivate a taste for minor music, it is indispensable to high attainments in the art.

**No. 513.**  You will remember that the *s* indicates the first inversion, and ↓ the second inversion of the common chord; also, that ↓ indicates the first, ↓ the second, and ↓ the third inversions of the chord of the seventh.  You will also keep in mind that ↓ or the absence of figures indicate the common chord direct; also, that a sharp, flat, or natural alone, or over or under a figure, always refers to the third.  In naming these chords describe them quite fully, as, tonic common chord direct, tonic common chord first inversion, &c.  When you come to the chord of D in the fourth measure, say "dominant in G common chord," the next will be tonic in G, but the next being a chord of the seventh will of course be a dominant chord, and by it you return to the key of C.

**No. 514.**  Before reminding you of what your teacher tells you about ↓↓ it will be well to give you a tabular view of the full figuring of these chords, together with their abbreviations.

Common chord direct full figuring ↓, abbreviation, either figure, or no figures.            Chord of the seventh first inversion ↓, abbreviation ↓.

Common chord first inversion ↓, abbreviation *s*.                                               Chord of the seventh second inversion ↓, abbreviation ↓.

Common chord second inversion ↓, abbreviation ↓.                                               Chord of the seventh third inversion ↓, abbreviation ↓.

Chord of the seventh direct ↓, abbreviation *r*.                                               Chord of the ninth direct ↓, abbreviation ↓.

Now if each base note were fully figured, you could play just as correctly by reckoning the intervals from the base note according to the figures,—for example where ↓, is written, a third, fifth and eighth will give you the common chord direct, so when ↓ is written, a sixth, third and eighth will give you the first inversion of the common chord, but, remember that in this way of finding out chords you reckon from the *written base note*, which you know is not always one, as we have been regarding the chords.  If therefore you reckon this ↓↓ from the base note you will find you have the second inversion of the chord of the seventh of E, the sharp sixth from the base note being the major third in the dominant seventh chord of this key.  It may be well, also, to remind you that chords are often named from their figuring.  The first inversion of the common chord being called the chord of the sixth, the second inversion the chord of six four, &c.

**No. 515.**  Notice that the second chord in **the** second measure is dominant in the key of D major, and that the chords in the fifth measure are dominant chords in E minor,—when you name these latter say "dominant in the relative minor."  Can you tell at what chord you are fairly back into G major?  The natural before the seventh indicates the dominant seventh in C, and so you go out of the key again.  What would a seventh from G be in this key?  Would F sharp in the chord of the seventh of G be pleasant?  You see then why the natural is placed before the seven here.  You will probably have no difficulty in discovering that the next chord is a suspension of the common chord of C, being indicated by ↓ and followed by ↓.

**No. 516.**  Remember that the chord of the ninth is formed by adding a ninth to the chord of the seventh, meaning of course a ninth from the base note.  At the third measure of this brace, say, "tonic in the relative minor," &c.  Persist in making yourself thoroughly familiar with all the chords, in all the keys.

**No. 517.** Remember that dashes are substitutes for previous figures or accidentals, and that single figures, like the last (87) mean that only one part should move—that the other tones should be held while the 8th and 7th are given.

**No. 518.**

**No. 519.** What does a natural under the base note signify? What does a natural before the 6 signify? What chord is $\frac{6}{4}$ the full figuring of? You perceive that the change from the major to the minor, and *vice versa*, in the same lesson, is easily made.

**No. 520.** What tone is a seventh from E flat according to this signature? What tones are necessary to make the chord of the seventh of E flat (the dominant seventh in the key of A flat)? You perceive by this why the flat is placed before the 7 here in the last measure but one.

**No. 221.** You observe that when a base note is not figured, and yet cannot be the base of the common chord, it must be a passing note.

**No. 222.**

**No. 523.** Be careful to sing these exercises in the key best adapted to the compass of your voice. Use syllables and vowel sounds.

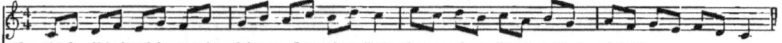

**No. 524.** Take breath but once in each lesson. Low voices will sing these exercises well in G, A flat, A. and B flat.

**No. 525.** High voices will do well to take these exercises in D flat, D, or E flat.

**No. 526.**

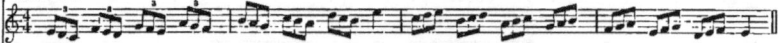

**No. 527.** Do not attempt to sing so fast as to render the execution labored or indistinct.

**No. 528.** Remember that rapidity in vocal execution, like that of the fingers, is of gradual growth.

**No. 529.**

**No. 530.**

**No. 531.**

**No. 532.**

**No. 533.** Sing either part, or both if you have the requisite compass.

**No. 534.** SHOCK OF THE GLOTTIS.

**No. 535.** If you cannot take the tones easily in this way, practice on a single sound.

**No. 536.** Do not fail in each of these lessons to give variety to them by means of *p.*, *f.*, cres., dim, &c.

**No. 537.** It will be an excellent plan to transpose each of these lessons into at least one other key.

**No. 538.**

**No. 539.**

**No. 540.** You see that you are left to finish this exercise without aid from the book. It will be a good plan also to practice all these lessons continuing them an octave or two higher and lower than they are here written.

**No. 541.**  Practice also the melodic minor scale, and make still another by ascending like the harmonic and descending like the melodic.

**No. 542.**

**No. 543.**

**No. 544.**

**No. 545.**

**No. 546.**

No. 547.

No. 548.

No. 549.

No. 550.

**No. 553.** Double Dotted Notes.

**No. 554.**      ÉTUDES PROGRESSIVES.—The Woodland Ramble.

Name the chords of which these arpeggios are formed.  Also the modulations that take place.  Give the *leggiero* and other expression as perfectly as possible.  Look over again from page 36 to page 69, and see what chords these lessons are composed of.

**No. 555.**        SOLFEGGIO EIGHT.

Name first the chords with their inversions of which the accompaniment is made, then the modulations that take place in the piece.  Try first a plaintive and rather gentle expression—then one of more courage and boldness.  In the latter you will have to disregard in some places the marks of expression.  It is presumed that you can transpose this if it is not adapted to your voice in this key.

**No. 556.** Various Arpeggios of the Common Chord.

Play the following lessons according to this model, which is No. 556 printed in full, that is, play with *both hands*, making a part for the left hand an octave below the right,—the fingering for the left hand will be found under the music. Play each measure *three times* and then a longer tone on the note with which you commenced, to make the rhythmical section complete, and to end well. Make the fingers work as independently of the hand as possible. Accent the first tone of each group.

(No. 556 as it is to be played.)

No. 556.

No. 557.

No. 558.

No. 559.

No. 560.

No. 561.

No. 562.

No. 563.

No. 564.

No. 565.

No. 566.

No. 567.

No. 568.

No. 569.

No. 570.

No. 571.

No. 572.

No. 573.

No. 574.

No. 575.

No. 576.

No. 577.

No. 578.

No. 579.

**No. 580.**    ÉTUDES PROGRESSIVES.---Sprites of Shadow and Sunshine.

You perceive that the movement which produces an agitated and disturbed effect in the minor is simply gay and lively in the relative major.

**No. 581.**    ÉTUDES PROGRESSIVES.---The Sighing of the Breeze.

No. 582. No. 583.

No. 584. No. 585.

No. 586. No. 587.

No. 588.

No. 589.

No. 590.

21

**No. 591**                    SOLFEGGIO NINE.

You are now left to select your own places for taking breath, and thus to make the phrasing. Do not disturb the meaning and good effect of the music by taking breath in wrong places. You will find that you do not always have time to fill the lungs full.

**No. 592.** Sequences.

Vary the expression,—soft, loud, cres., dim., legato, and staccato. Transpose into another key if you can: it will be difficult. Endeavor to have the control and mastery of every note in each lesson from the begining: undertake only what you can perform, and then commence slow enough.

**No. 593.** Observe the directions given above. This will not be so difficult to transpose, and should be played in at least three other keys. Is your playing neat? It is far better to play slow, than to have your music confused, indistinct, or clumsy.

**No. 594.** Various Arpeggios of the Chord of the Seventh.

Play each measure three times with a long tone to close with, on the plan of No. 556. Play the proper tonic chord at the close of each lesson. These exercises will amply repay you for all the time and attention that you will give them.

No. 594.

No. 595.

No. 596.

No. 597.

No. 598.

No. 599.

No. 600.

No. 601.

No. 602.

No. 603.

Which way is the transposition here, by fifths or by fourths? It is because we hope you now play well enough to see the importance of technics that we give you so many to practice.

**No. 604.**

**No. 605.**

**No. 606.**

**No. 607.**

**No. 608.**

**No. 609.**

**No. 610.**

**No. 611.**

**No. 612.**

**No. 613.**

**No. 614.**

**No. 615.**

**No. 616.**    ÉTUDES PROGRESSIVES.---Sounds from the Chapel.

Keep the melody as connected as possible and strike the accompaniment neatly. Think while you play whether you are in major or minor, also whether you are in tonic, dominant or subdominant. If your piano is well in tune, and more especially if it sustains or vibrates well, you should derive considerable pleasure from the effort to make the melody sound like a voice. There is no objection to adding your voice here sometimes, making use of "ah," or the syllables la, si, do, &c.

**No. 617.**    ÉTUDES PROGRESSIVES.---Flashes on the Evening Cloud.

This étude is characterised by delicacy rather than power. Notice the repeat of two measures. It is necessary to the correct rythmic form.

**No. 618.** SOLFEGGIO TEN.

If you were to apply syllables here you would have no occasion to change their application in the little minor phrases, as they are applied to relative major and minor alike. Do not take breath between the 4th and 5th measures. This style of passing from one phrase to the next should be well learned.

**No. 619.** This exercise is regarded by some of the best teachers living, as second to none in importance. Play *each scale* major and minor, accenting in the four ways here given. You will now perceive the absolute necessity of knowing all the scales and their fingering by heart, but this we hope is accomplished. Play the unaccented notes lightly, that the accented ones may be prominent. Adhere to the right fingering.

**No. 620.** Accent all through as indicated at the beginning. Do not let the accenting throw you off from the right fingering. Play all the scales.

**No. 621.**

**No. 622.** Remember that the first note of each group should have a clear, prompt accent given with the *right finger*, and that the others should be rather light. -You should now know all the scales by heart, that you may transpose readily.

**No. 623.** Transpose this also into all the keys, major and minor, observing carefully the fingering of each scale. If you have been thorough in all the preceding lessons, it is believed that you will accomplish this transposing with only a moderate amount of effort. If you have not, it will be formidable.

Observe the directions given for fingering the arpeggios not here printed, and play them in their order.

**No. 624.**

C fingered like this.

**No. 625.**

A and E fingered like this.

**No. 626.**

**No. 627.** G♭ same as this. G♭ and F♯ fingered like C.

**No. 628.**

A♭ and E♭ fingered like this.

**No. 629.**

F fingered like C.

**No. 630.**                    SOLFEGGIO ELEVEN.

Do not neglect to sing these solfeggios sometimes with the other vowel sounds, and if your pronunciation needs improving, with the syllables.

ALLEGRETTO.

No. 631. Do you know the fingering?

No. 632.

No. 633.

No. 634. Both hands.

No. 635.

No. 636. Both hands. Ascend two octaves and descend the same.

**No. 637.**              ÉTUDES PROGRESSIVES.—Kitty by the Fireside.

CADENZA.  You perceive that your great work just now is the practice of technics or daily exercises.  These études and solfeggios are however of great importance, as they appeal to the taste and imagination.  Make them perfect.  This piece must, as you see, go quite fast when it is learned ; the chromatic groups should be very smoothly and closely linked together, if you would make it a good musical picture.  With a little aid of the imagination the contented purring of this favorite of the household may here be quite pleasantly represented.

### ÉTUDES PROGRESSIVES.—Sadness, Hope, Joy.

**No. 638.**   You may substitute other expressions for those indicated here, if you can by that means make the music more descriptive of the emotions spoken of in the title.

**No. 639.**              SOLFEGGIO TWELVE.

Notice that after observing the first Da Capo, you play the section in C minor, and after repeating that so as to give its second ending, you D. C. again to close with.   Pass from the last tone of the minor section to the beginning in the D. C. without taking breath.

This has been well called by some authors THE GRAND PRACTICE OF THE SCALES. No technics are on the whole so important as these, especially if they include the various accents and other expressions. You have here the model of each key, major and minor; practice equally in all. Not only should these technics form daily exercises until they are mastered, but they should be continued as long as you wish to keep yourself in the practice of the piano-forte. Begin slow enough to have the fingering perfect, and the touch clear and neat. Finger as in the other scales.

**No. 640.**

**No. 641.**

**No. 642.** Both hands.

**No. 643.**

**No. 644.**

**No. 645.**

**No. 646.**

**No. 647.**

**No. 648.**

**No. 649.**

**No. 650.**

**No. 651.**

**No. 652.**          ÉTUDES PROGRESSIVES.—Apprehension, Suspense, Certainty.

Remember that before you can give your imagination free play in these études, the mechanical part of the work of playing them must be very perfect.  Time, fingering, accents, &c., must be so mastered that you seem to give them scarcely a thought.  Into how many keys does the lesson go?

## ÉTUDES PROGRESSIVES.—The return of the Regiment,

**No. 653.**   The principal mechanical difficulty here is in the wrist motion.   Do not play so fast as to make this irregular or indistinct.   It is hoped that these harmonies are now so familiar to you, that your thoughts can be given to the subject you wish to describe, and the emotion you wish to express. After observing the first Da Capo, omit the second section, and play the third—then D. C. to close with.

**No. 654.**  Play this through all the keys, transposing by fourths.  You observe that the same fingering is used in each ascending group in the right hand and reversing, the same in descending.  So in the left.  Adhere to this fingering in all the keys.

Transpose into all the keys, major and minor.  It is necessary to know the fingering by heart.

**No. 655.**

**No. 656.**

**No. 657.**

Play this exercise with the same fingering in G major, F major, and F sharp major; also in A minor, E minor, D minor and E flat minor.

**No. 658.**

Play this exercise with the same fingering in A major and E major; also in G minor, C minor and F minor.

**No. 659.**

**No. 660.**

**No. 661.**

Play this exercise with the same fingering in E flat major, in A flat major and D flat major.

**No. 662.**

**No. 663.**

**No. 664.**     ÉTUDES PROGRESSIVES.—Dance of the Rustic Masqueraders.

It is only when you can play this étude perfectly in time and tune that you will be ready to practice to bring out or develop its musical meaning—a most important part of your musical education. Do not make the first three notes in the base a triplet—join them to the first note in the treble as though they all formed one group of four. To what key does the modulation here take place? What is the tone of modulation.

**No. 665.**  **ÉTUDES PROGRESSIVES.—The Chase of the Chamois.**

These études will be interesting to your friends and useful to yourself, only as they are thoroughly played, and their meaning fully brought out; many excellent pieces are pronounced uninteresting simply because they are not understood, or are not well played.

**No. 666.**  Play this sometimes even—sometimes accenting the first of each two, and sometimes *cres.* ascending, and *dim.* descending.

**No. 667.**  Observe the directions given above for this, with the exception of the accent which should be on the first of each three.

**No. 668.**     ÉTUDES PROGRESSIVES.—The Wind among the Forest Trees,

A certain degree of velocity will be necessary here to produce the right effect, but the commencement of the practice should be, as in all cases, slow, distinct and perfect.  While practicing this étude let the memory call to mind the various fitful sounds of the wind in the forest, and let the imagination clothe the music with a corresponding expression.  Work patiently to get this left hand part perfect.

**No. 669.**    Be careful to accent the first note of each group of two, and make the second staccato.  You perceive that this lesson is abbreviated. Can you supply the deficiency?  You will do well to play it also in the key of D flat, observing the same fingering.

### No. 670. Supertonic, Mediant, Submediant and Leading note. Imperfect Common Chord.

Before playing this lesson play the common chord belonging to each tone of the major scale, using no chromatic tones. Do this in every major scale. How many kinds of common chords have we? What are the intervals of the major common chord? What of the minor? What of the imperfect? What kind of a common chord is found upon the tonic in any major key? What upon the supertonic? What upon the mediant? What upon the subdominant? What upon the dominant? What upon the submediant? What upon the leading note? Transpose into all the keys and name the chords here as you play, as, chord of the tonic, chord of the subdominant, chord of the supertonic, and continue naming them through all the keys. It is believed that you now have but little difficulty in transposing. If this is not so, you are earnestly advised to go over the lessons in transposition again.

*First transposition.*

### No. 671. New Chords of the Seventh.

Before playing this lesson play the chord of the seventh on each tone of the scale, using no chromatic tones. Examine and name the intervals forming these chords. How many different chords of the seventh do you find? You will find them more agreeable in the lesson than when played separately.

*First transposition.*

### No. 672. The use of the Common Chords on the Submediant, Supertonic and Mediant.

Do not fail here to become familiar with the new things and their names, supertonic, mediant, &c., so that when it is said, for example, that the mediant is rarely used, except in its first inversion, the phrase shall not seem as if it was in an unknown tongue, but familiar and clear,—a moderate amount of effort on your part will surely accomplish this. Your teacher will tell you how to work if the right way does not occur to you. The chords of the submediant, and supertonic, of any major key, are the same as the tonic, and subdominant of its relative minor, and may be used in either way although it is not usual to regard them as in the minor while performing a major piece, unless the phrase in which they occur is mostly minor. This cadence illustrates the most common use of the submediant, supertonic, and mediant chords,—the submediant being mostly found in its direct form, the supertonic generally in its first inversion, though sometimes direct, while the mediant is almost never used excepting in its first inversion and in this particular way. It will be an excellent plan to play these lessons in various arpeggio forms like those on page 117.

### No. 673. Use of the Common Chord on the leading note, and the Chord of the 7th on the Supertonic.

This cadence shows the most common use of the chord of the leading note, and the chord of the 7th, with the minor third,—the latter being the supertonic chord, and both in the first inversion. These lessons should all be learned by heart, and should be played as well in one key as another.

### No. 674. Resolutions of the Chords of the Seventh.

Play the chord of the dominant seventh in each key, and make it resolve to the submediant. This progression you will frequently find in both vocal and instrumental music.

**No. 675.** The Chord of the Diminished Seventh, and its Resolutions.

Before playing this lesson, play the chord of the dominant seventh direct in the key of C, and then by a change only of the lower tone make a chord of the diminished seventh. Do this in every other major (or minor) key. What intervals make this chord? Do you notice that going from one tone to the next, in the chord of the diminished seventh you have successively the same interval? Play it with one hand so as to bring the tones nearer together, and you will perceive it with the eye, and perhaps with the ear, which is more important. Of how many half steps is this interval composed? (You will find that this interval is sometimes represented to the eye as an augmented second, and sometimes as a minor third.) Since then there is but one kind of interval in this chord (reckoning from one tone to the next,) and that interval composed of only three half steps, it follows that there can really be but three different chords of the diminished seventh, just as there can be but one chromatic scale, because there is but one kind of interval in it, and that composed of only one-half step. You will notice, however, that these three chords are both written and resolved differently as they occur in the different keys. After playing perhaps you will notice that the second chord in this little lesson in C, the fourth in the lesson in D, the second in A, the fourth in B, the second in F♯, the second (of course) in G♮, the fourth in A♭, the second in E♮, and the fourth in F, are all to the ear the same chord, only with different representations, and different resolutions, and in different positions. Please point out the different places of the other two. An excellent plan to help you in understanding and forming these chords will be to produce a succession of minor thirds from any tone, say C; then give them both in chord and in arpeggio form,—do the same commencing with C♯, then the same commencing with D, and you have all; for if you commence with E♭, you must produce an inversion of the first, and with E, an inversion of the second, &c. You perceive that in this lesson we not only have the chord of the diminished seventh that is founded as it were on the dominant in each key, but also the one that would occur in the same place in the next key, (transposing by fifths,) and that the latter resolves in a different way from the former. Is the first chord of the diminished seventh in each key here, direct or inverted? The second? Which inversion? See how many pleasant resolutions you can play to each of these three chords?

Fill up the gap in the transposition of this cadence by playing it also in B, F♯, G♭, D♭, and A♭.

**No. 676.** The Chord of the Extended Sixth.

This chord which is considerably used in the music of the present day, will perhaps be better understood by considering it the second inversion of the dominant seventh of the next key, (transposing by fifths,) only the base note is flatted, and the fourth sharped (so to speak,) thus making it resolve very differently from what it otherwise would. It may seem strange to you that there should be a fourth in the chord of the seventh, but this phraseology, like the term "extended sixth," is derived from the marking for thorough base. What intervals make this chord?

Play this also in G, E, B, F♯, G♭, D♮, and A♭.

It is believed that you will now be able to tell at every modulation into what key you go, and also the tones by which the change is made. It is not thought necessary to classify all the modulations that may be made. Analyze and name carefully all the harmony of every piece you play and sing, before performing it.

## No. 677.                    ÉTUDES ÉLÉGANTES.—L'Angelus.

A careless playing of this, and of some other pieces that follow, may perhaps give you the idea that they are easy, and that they should have been practiced at an early stage of this Curriculum.    You will, however, probably change your mind when you undertake to give every tone here indicated its *exact value*, no more, no less, and the melody its cantabile character.    Difficulties in piano-forte playing do not always exist in rapid execution.    Some of the most subtle and troublesome are of this unobtrusive kind, and require not only great control of the fingers in a certain way, but considerable taste and musical culture.    It is, therefore, not always wise to pronounce a piece easy because at the first glance it looks so.

CANTABILE.                                                                                                    F. Hünten.

No. 678.                    SONGS OF THE WANDERER.—Mother.

1. O 'tis rest    here to sit    by your side    Moth-er dear,    In your
2. Now of child - hood I dream    once a - gain    Moth-er dear,    Of its
3. Let your hand    rest a - gain    on my head    Moth-er dear,    As 'twas

love    O 'tis sweet    to con - fide    Moth-er dear,    In the gay    world I've    met    with the
haunts    in the wild - wood and glen    Moth-er dear,    When I wan - der'd    till    warn'd    by the
wont    when you knelt - by my bed    Moth-er dear.    And the peace    that    was    mine    in the

wel - come    and    smile,    But my heart    grew more    lone - ly    and    wea - ry    the    while.    So 'tis rest    here to
dark - ness    and    dew,    When I turn'd    me    as    now    to my    home    and    to    you.    O 'tis rest    here to
mo - ments    so    bright,    Shall re - turn    now    to    calm and    to    bless    me    to - night.    O 'tis rest    here to

sit    by your side    Moth-er    dear,    In your love    O 'tis sweet    to con - fide    Moth-er    dear.
sit    by your side    Moth-er    dear,    In your love    O 'tis sweet    to con - fide    Moth-er    dear.
sit    by your side    Moth-er    dear,    In your love    O 'tis sweet    to con - fide    Moth-er    dear.

**No. 679.** Syncopation, Second Form.

First play without the ties, then with them, counting promptly.    Think of the two tied eighths as making a quarter.

**No. 680.**

MODERATO.                    ÉTUDES PROGRESSIVES.----The Merry Blacksmith.

**No. 681.** Skips in Left Hand.    Name the chords and inversions formed by the left hand.

**No. 682.  Turn and Mordente.**

You perceive that the embellishments here used are first written out in full, and then indicated by their usual signs.  You will notice that when the sign of the turn is placed exactly *over* a note it indicates a different effect from what it does when placed between notes.  You will also observe that there are little differences in the form and sound of the turn, these are to be regulated by your taste.  It may be proper here to say that embellishments are now-a-days frequently indicated in full either as here by large notes, or, by the use of the little grace notes.  Play the melody first, beginning at the second section, *without* observing the signs of embellishment—afterwards the whole piece, not too fast.

**No. 683.  Pedal Harmony.**

Observe that this lesson is first played through with the usual harmony, then with pedal harmony.   After a time the latter will be preferred.

ANDANTINO.

**No. 684.**                    **ÉTUDES ÉLÉGANTES.--Le Chanson du Matin.**

In this étude some of the turns are indicated by appoggiaturas—notes which have no value of their own, but borrow from their neighbors.   This mode of indicating the turn is frequently employed,—notice the pedal harmony in the third measure.   What chord would be used commonly?   Try it. Which do you like best?   Can you tell to what keys the little modulations here take you?   Say which are tones of chords, and which are passing notes. A considerable difficulty in this piece consists in giving an accent to the first note of the short legato marks, making the last one short and soft, and linking closely all that are connected.

A. Loeschorn.

Il basso marcato.

**No. 685.** ÉTUDES ÉLÉGANTES.—Souvenir d'Enfance.

Endeavor to understand all the chords, and into what keys you modulate. Observe the rule for the legato marks first given. *A. Loeschorn.*

♩=128.

Arpeggios of the Chords of the Diminished Seventh.   Play the unfinished lessons like the complete ones.

No. 686.

No. 687.          No. 688.          No. 689.

No. 690.

No. 691.          No. 692.          No. 693.

No. 694.

No. 695.          No. 696.          No. 697.

No. 698.          SONGS OF THE WANDERER.---Retrospection.

1. O si - lent night, so calm and still, Thy shad - ows fall on wood and hill............ Con-
2. And while up - on the scene I gaze, A bright form comes from out the maze............ And

ceal - ing from the wand - 'rers sight Those scenes of child - hood's dear de - light, Thro'
fol - lowing on my way - ward track, With gen - tle love al - lures me back. But

mem - 'ry's long past years I turn, And lights on ev - 'ry hill - top burn, And in the
now the vis - ion slow - ly fades, The fires are lost in mem - 'ry's shades, And night a -

wind - ing paths I see The hap - py child I used to be.
gain so calm and still, Her shad - ows flings o'er wood and hill.

**No. 699.**           ÉTUDES CARACTÉRISTIQUES.---Song without words.

The pupil will observe that the main difficulty in this lesson, consists in connecting the melody, and in making it sound as much as possible like a voice.  Give well the gradual modulations indicated by the dynamic marks.

## No. 700. The Trill.

You observe that the trill is the rapid alternation of a tone indicated by a written note, with the one a step or half step above it, and that you commence the trill sometimes with the upper and sometimes with the lower of these two tones—that it has a turn at the close to give it a finish, excepting in certain descending phrases, and that it must be *in time*, having just four or eight tones to a count (excepting sometimes in the turn). Notice also that in some cases an appoggiatura precedes the trill when it commences with the lower tone. Play the piece thoroughly, giving four tones to each count in the trill, then try eight, as indicated in the group of choice notes. Ascertain carefully the right fingering.

**No. 701.**  Octaves.

Turn back to page 45, and commence at No. 16 for your "Twenty-fifth series of instrumental exercises for daily practice." Play this series and as many more as your teacher thinks best, in octaves, striking from the wrist as much as possible.

**No. 702.**        ÉTUDES CARACTÉRISTIQUES,—Polonaise.

ALLEGRETTO.                                                                        Emil Rein.

**No. 703.**        ÉTUDES ÉLÉGANTES.—Le Printemps.

♩=88.                                                                              A. Loeschorn.

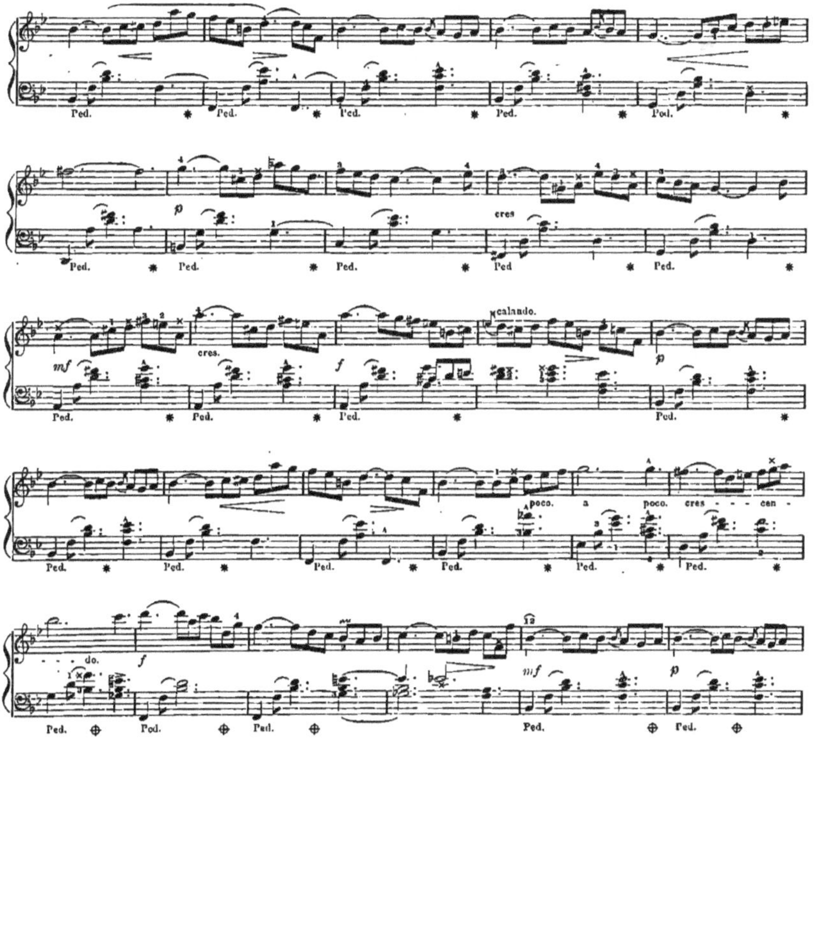
Ped.
cres
mf
cres.
f
calando.
p
poco. a poco. cres - - - cen -
- - - do.
mf

**No. 704.**    SONGS OF THE WANDERER.---The Absent One.

1. Where is May,    sis - ter May    that I    loved    so    well?    It was here,    just    here    that she said    fore-
2. In the thought    of my home    from a    far    off    land,    It was here,    just    here    that I    saw    her
3. I have sought    thee my home,    Oh a    wea - ry    guest,    When the bird    has    flown    do we    heed    the

well.    Oh    her dancing feet were ev - er    first to meet me, And her lit - tle hands to cling to    mine.    Ev-ery    sun-ny smile    and
stand.    Oh    her lov-ing glan - ces beam'd up-on my com-ing With the light of oth - er hap - py    days.    And the beauteous form    so
nest!    But    my darling sis - ter    in her    an - gel radiance Yet shall greet me with her lov-ing    kiss.    For she's watching in    her

artless word shall    mem'ry e'er    en - shrine.    Why so    still    and    sad?    Why    look    a - way!    O
full of love    on - tranced my rap - turous    gaze.    Art thou here    sweet    one?    Oh    say    not    nay.    O
bright home as    she watch'd for me    in    this.    Why so    still!    and    sad?    Why    turn    a - way!    O

where,    O    where    is    May    dear    May,    O    where,    O    where    is    May    dar-ling May!
where,    O    where    is    May    dear    May,    O    where,    O    where    is    May    dar-ling May?
there,    O    there    is    May    dear    May,    O    there,    O    there    is    May    dar-ling May.

No. 705.

ÉTUDES ÉLÉGANTES.---L' Été.

A. Loeschorn.

**No. 706.**                    ÉTUDES PROGRESSIVES.---The Bees in the Heather Bells.

Connect well, and make somewhat prominent, the melody formed by the eighth notes. This will be done by giving them a little accent.

1st time.
2d time.
ritard.
a tempo.
cres.
dim.
dim. e ritard
p
m
f
mf
pp
ppp

**No. 707.** In this exercise make a part for the left hand by playing an octave below the right.  Its fingering is under the lesson.  Play each

**No. 708.**        **No. 709.**

**No. 710.**        **No. 711.**

**No. 712.**        **No. 713.**

**No. 714.**        **No. 715.**

**No. 716.**        **No. 717.**

measure ten times.　F and II may be played together, as may G and I.　Strike the notes exactly together.　Vary the exercises.　Transpose.

**F** Right hand.　**G** Right hand.　**II** Left hand.　**I** Left hand.

No. 718.　　　　No. 719.

No. 720.　　　　No. 721.

No. 722.　　　　No. 723.

No. 724.　　　　No. 725.

No. 726.　　　　No. 727.

**No. 728.**
GIOJOSO.

SONGS OF THE WANDERER.---The Welcome.

1. Hap-py the wa - king! Hap-py the wa - king, In the fair light of this beauti - ful morn; Dear ones are
2. Mer-ri-ly ring - ing! Mer-ri-ly ring - ing, Down in the glad heart the sweet bells of joy; "Meet we for
3. Tell o'er thy sor - row! Tell o'er thy sor - row, Knowing that thine it shall be nev - er-more, Sun-light is

com - ing, dear ones are com - ing, coming to wel - come the wan-der - er home. They gather, They
ev - er, meet we for - ev - er" are the blest words that the ech - oes em - ploy. Come hither, Come
bright - est, sun-light is bright - est when it has burst thro' the storm-bolted door. A - waken, A-

gath-er, The joy - ful mu - sic hear. O wel-come, yes wel-come, To friends and neigh-bors
hith-er, O car - ol, car - ol now— Ye songsters, Ye songsters From ev - ery woodland
wa-ken, The wild-est gladdest strain, O wel-come, O wel-come Be - lov - ed ones a-

dear. Hap - py the wak - ing, hap-py the wak - ing, In the fair light of this beau - ti - ful
bough. Mer - ri - ly ring - ing, mer - ri - ly ring - ing, Down in the glad heart the sweet bells of
gain. Tell o'er thy sor - row, tell o'er thy sor - row, Know-ing that thine it can be nev - er

morn,        Dear ones are com  -  ing,  dear ones are com  -  ing,  Com-ing to  wel  -  come the wan-der - er  home.
joy,        "Meet  we for - ev  -  er,  meet we for - ev - er,"  These are the words  that  the  ech - oes em - ploy.
more,       Sun - light is  bright  -  est,  sunlight is  bright  -  est,  When it hath burst  thro' the storm bolt-ed  door.

No. 729.                ÉTUDES PROGRESSIVES.---The Rippling Brook.
♩=112                                                                    J. Concone.

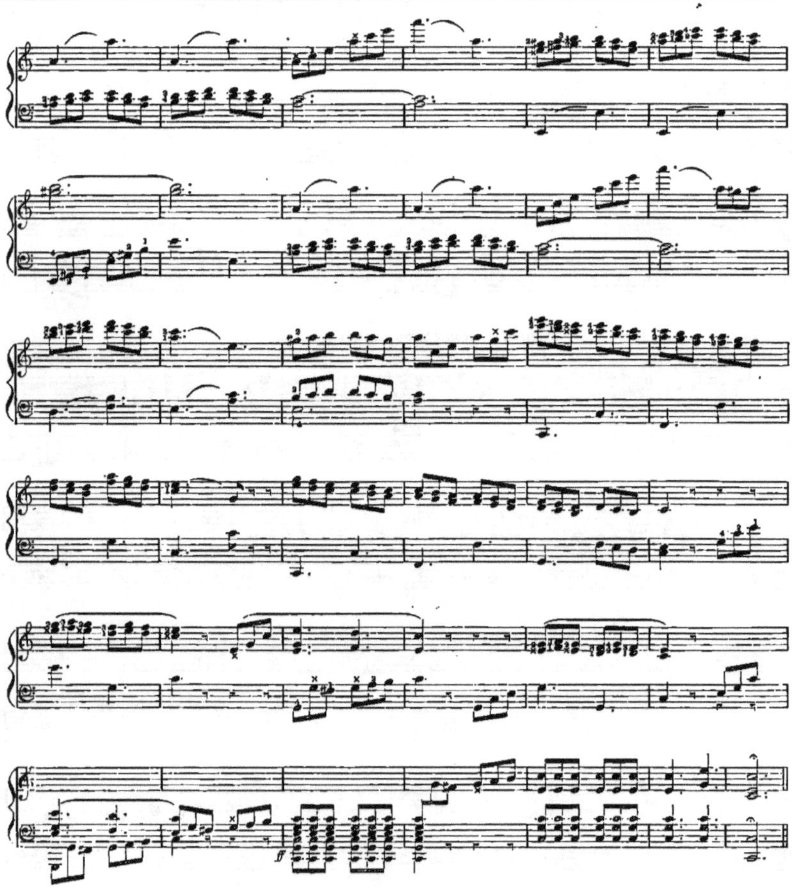

**No. 730.**                    ÉTUDES CARACTÉRISTIQUES.—Nocturne.

                                                      *Emil Reis.*

Each of the Études Caractéristiques, you perceive, is a specimen of one of the more unusual kinds of music. The nocturne, or "music of the night," is usually of this singing, yet fanciful character. It is not expected that it will be as popular as some of the brighter music, but it will meet the wants of certain states of feeling, and will be sure to improve on acquaintance. All the pieces in this part of the book should be thoroughly analyzed that every harmony and every modulation may be known.

**No. 731.    SONGS OF THE WANDERER.---Reminiscences of the Battle-Field.**

1. O    yes to the battle field    In    tho't I go a-gain,    And    see in the silence there .    My comrades on the plain.    Then
2. A - way to the honor'd van!    A - way! ye brave a-way!    Let    him loi-ter now who can    To    look upon the fray ;    To

loud-ly the bu-gles sound,    And    fiercely rolls the drum    And    ere the command is giv'n    We know the hour has come:
note how anoth - er bears .    The    ban-ner staff in pride    To    dream where another's son    May boast his fath - er died..

Now    boys    on!    be    firm    and steady.    On,    boys,    on!    be strong    and true,
Now    boys    on!    one brave    endeav-or.    On,    boys,    on!    one hon - ored thrust,

Now    boys,    on!    let all    be read - y    for    the    work    that we    must do.    Ah
Now    boys,    on!    our cause    for ev - er,    See    their    flag    low in    the dust,    Oh

yes to the bat-tle field.    In thought I go a - gain,......    And    see    in the silence there    My comrades on the plain.
yes to the bat-tle field, &c.

(For intricate play pu-tu hr.)

No. 732.

ÉTUDES CARACTÉRISTIQUES.—Serenade.

Ch. Fradel.

ANDANTINO.

27

Ped.
cres.
rit.
il canto ben marcato.
rall.
1st time.
2d time.
p a tempo.
molto rit.
cres.
Fine.

After learning the scales in thirds, and these in sixths, you will be able, should your teacher think it best, to practice successfully the same in the various relative minors. It may be desirable for you to precede the practice of this page with exercises like A, B, F, G, H and I, on pages 202 and 203. If so, you can easily make them by *inverting* the tones of those very lessons.

No. 733.                    No. 734.

No. 735.                    No. 736.

No. 737.                    No. 738.

No. 739.                    No. 740.

No. 741.                    No. 742.

**No. 743.**    ÉTUDES PROGRESSIVES.—The Wild Horse on the Prairie.

Be careful to observe the repeats, and first and second endings; also the proper place for the final ending.    Strike with a flexible hand.

*Th. Kullack.*

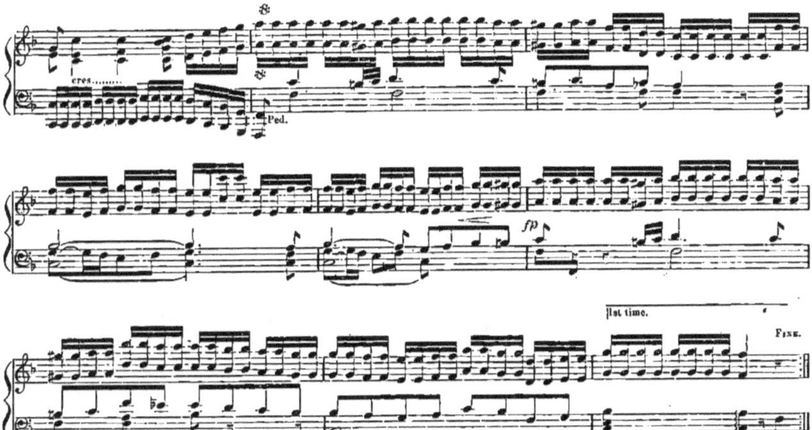
cres.........
Ped.
fp
1st time.
Fine.
2d time.
mf
DAL SEGNO.

**No. 744.**    **ÉTUDES ÉLÉGANTES.—La Frileuse.**

J. Concone

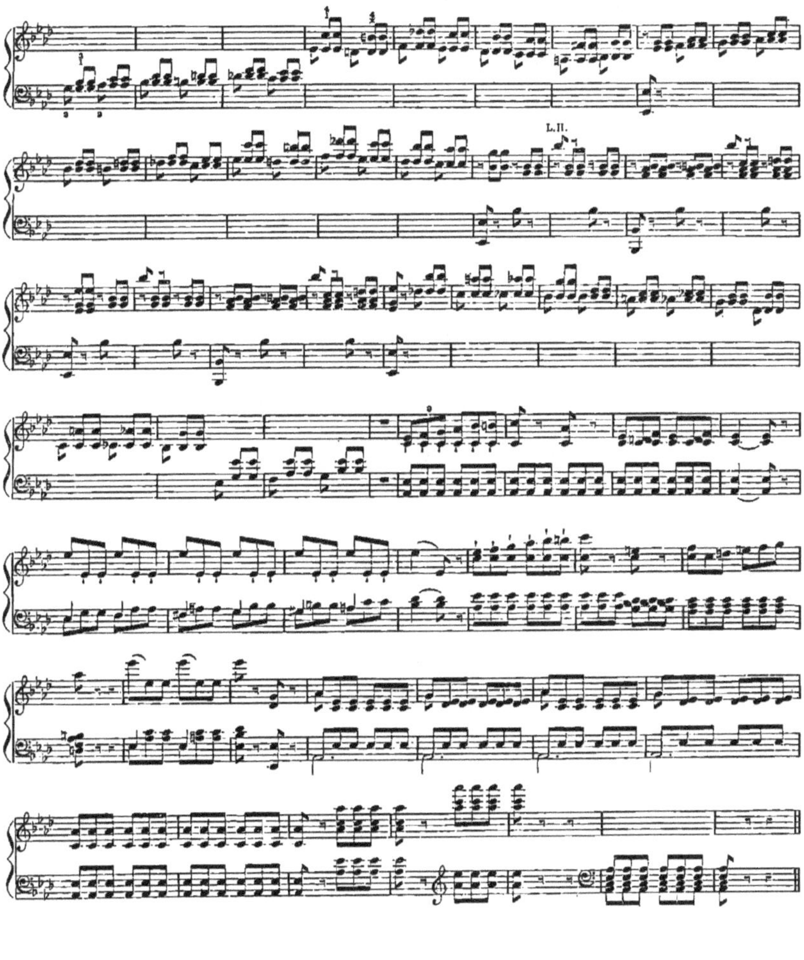
L. H.

**No. 745.**     SONGS OF THE WANDERER.---Songs of Home.

*Moderato.*

*Allegretto.*

1. Songs of home,   Songs of home!   How I love your well known strains, Round my heart, round my heart, Ye have bound your silver chains.
2. Songs of home,   Songs of home!   Tho' my feet have widely strayed, Ye re - call,   ye re - call   To the roof-tree's bless-ed shade.

For to you,   for to you,   on each dark and dreary day, Have I turned, have I turned while so far,   so far a - way.
For the heart,   for the heart,   while it glad - dens or it grieves, Like a bird, like a bird, seeks the same be - lov-ed eaves.

*Moderato.*

Oh yes there is   no spot on earth   so dear to me as home.   No fai - ry land   like thine to which my
Oh yes there is   no dear - er spot   this side the rest a - bove,   Than home with all   its hallowed ties of

heart so longed to come,   And where in - deed can love so true   and tones so sweet be   found...... As here a-mid the
ten-derness and love,   With ev - ery ten - dril in - ter - twined that frail ex - is - tence knows,   And hope and joy and

scenes and songs of childhoods charmed ground.  Home.  home, sweet  songs  of  home.  There are
grief combined as petals of a  rose.  Home,  home, sweet  songs  of  home.  There &c

no  strains so dear  as thine sweet songs of home.

**No. 746.**
*Vivo.* $\boldsymbol{\frown}$=160. 3
PRELUDE.

ÉTUDES ÉLÉGANTES.—Les Papillons.

*J. Concone.*

*leggieremente.*

*Allegretto.*

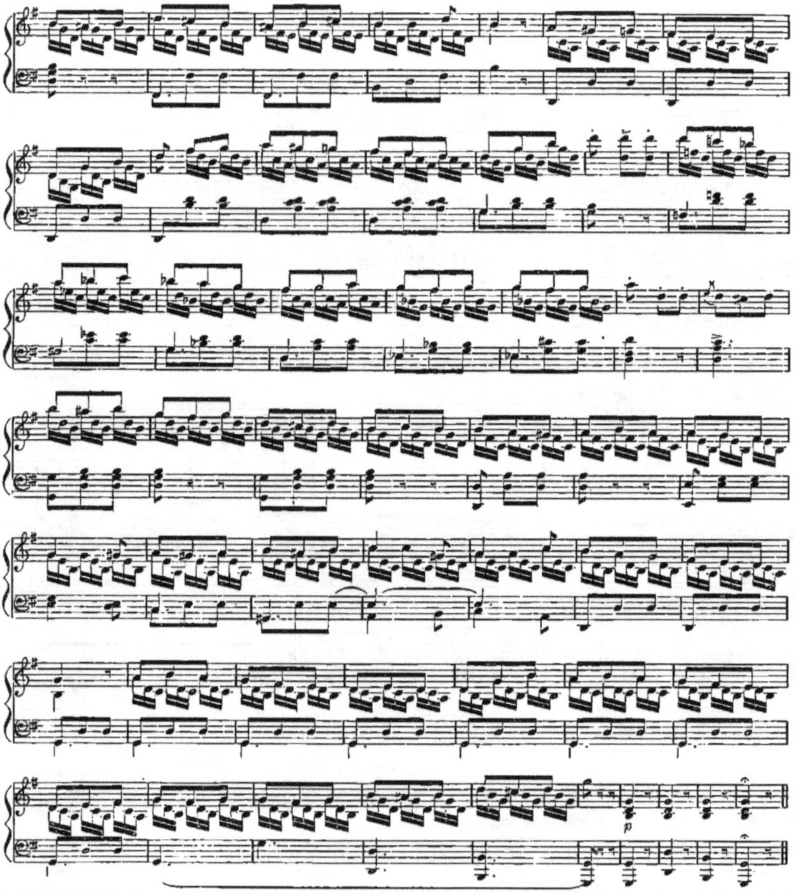
p

## No. 747. Tremolo, Measure repeat, Abbreviations.

It would be well to take the dampers off the strings by means of the pedal, during the continuance of each chord,—stopping the vibration where the chord changes. It is not uncommon in the tremolo to make the tremulous motion of the hand as fast as may be, keeping the general time of the measure, rather than attending to each note. Observe that the marks of abbreviation over the base at the ninth measure show that you are to play as at the beginning. Give the expression according to your own taste.

## No. 748.    ÉTUDES ÉLÉGANTES.—La Ronde des Archers.

A careful examination should be made of the chords, modulations, suspensions, passing notes and general style of these études, that they may be played from intelligence and appreciation.   It is expected that the pupil who learns everything thoroughly as he goes on in this Curriculum, will enjoy them; but it is not so certain that his friends, who have not had a similar training, will at first perceive their excellence—but to all they will improve.

PRELUDE.
Moderato quasi Allegretto. ♩=104.

J. Concone.

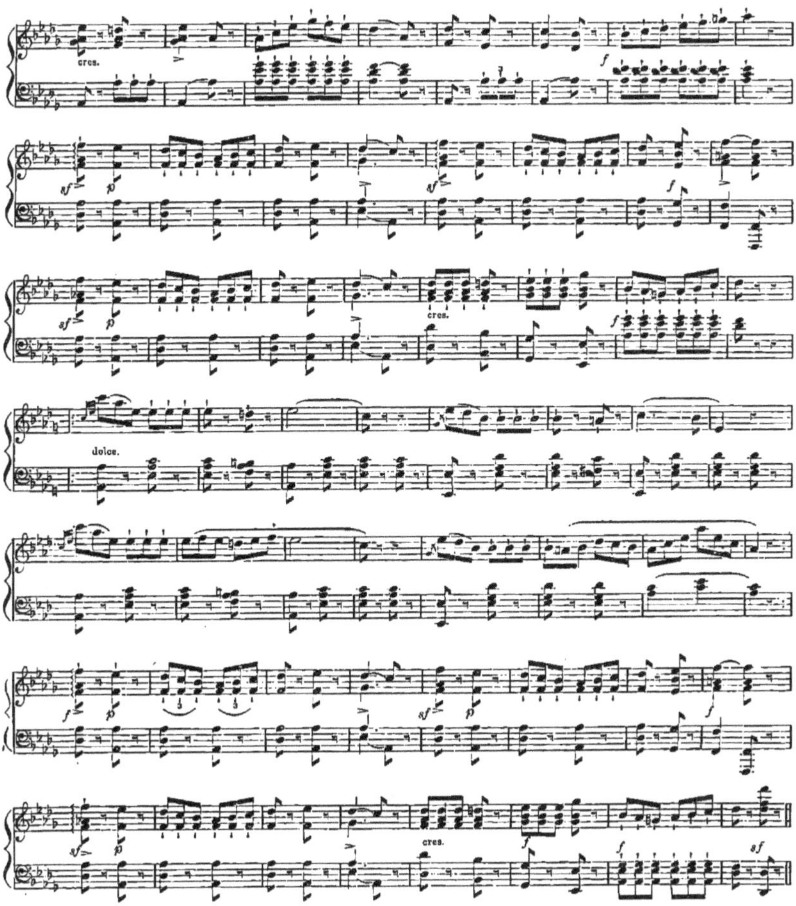
cres.
dolce.
cres.
cres.

No. 749.         ÉTUDES ÉLÉGANTES.—L'Hirondelle.

PRELUDE.
Vivo e leggiero. ♩=100.

J. Concone.

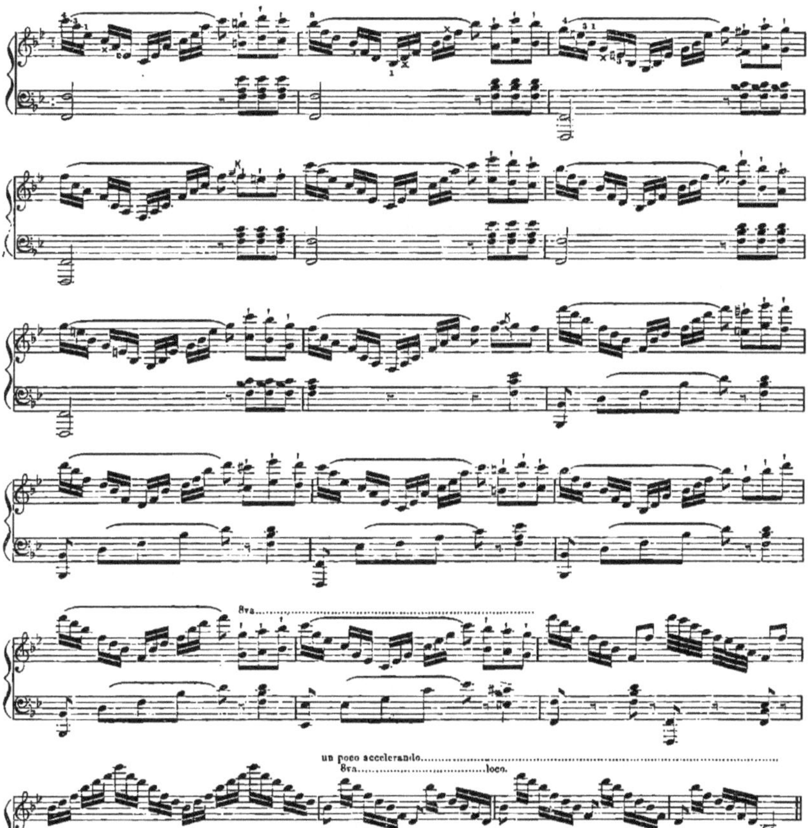
8va
un poco accelerando
8va
loco.

**No. 750.** These exercises include the practice of the Turn, and some preparation for the Shake. They also afford means for the practice of the

No. 751.

No. 752.

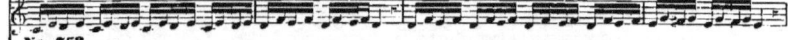

No. 753.

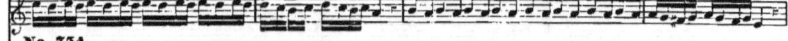

No. 754.

No. 755.

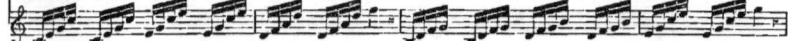

No. 756.

No. 757.

No. 758.

No. 759.

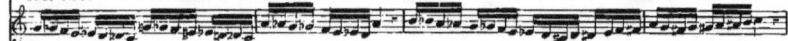

No. 760.

chromatic scale, and the arpeggios of major and minor common chords, as well as those of the dominant, and diminished sevenths. Use syllabics, and vowels.

**No. 761.**    ÉTUDES CARACTÉRISTIQUES.—Transcription.

The melody commences with the base clef, and rather slow.    The left hand crosses over the right.    The theme should sound like a baritone song.

J. Ch. Hess.

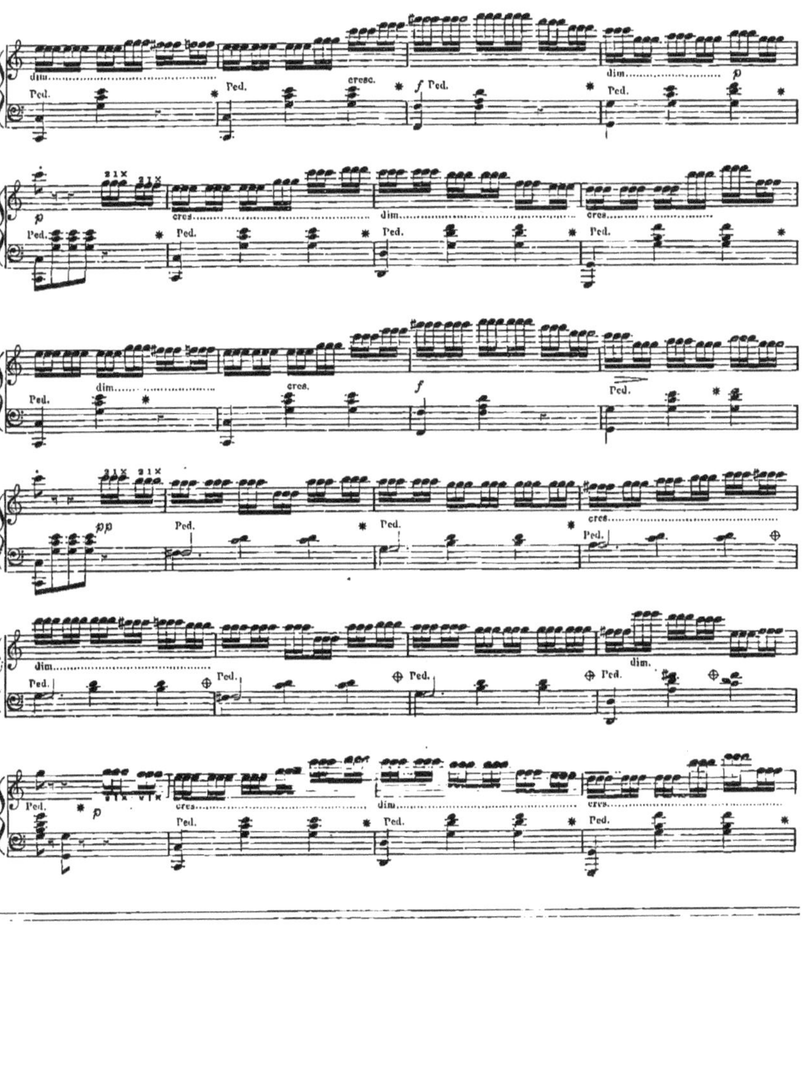
dim.
Ped.
cresc.
f
p
cres.
pp

**No. 762.**    **ÉTUDES ÉLÉGANTES.---Magic Bells.**    *Th. Oesten.*

fz
f
dim.
p
rit.
f a tempo.
8va...
cres.
8va....loco.
fz
dim.
p
cres.
fz
8va....loco.
ff

**No. 763.**            ÉTUDES CARACTÉRISTIQUES.—Reverie.

D. Krug.

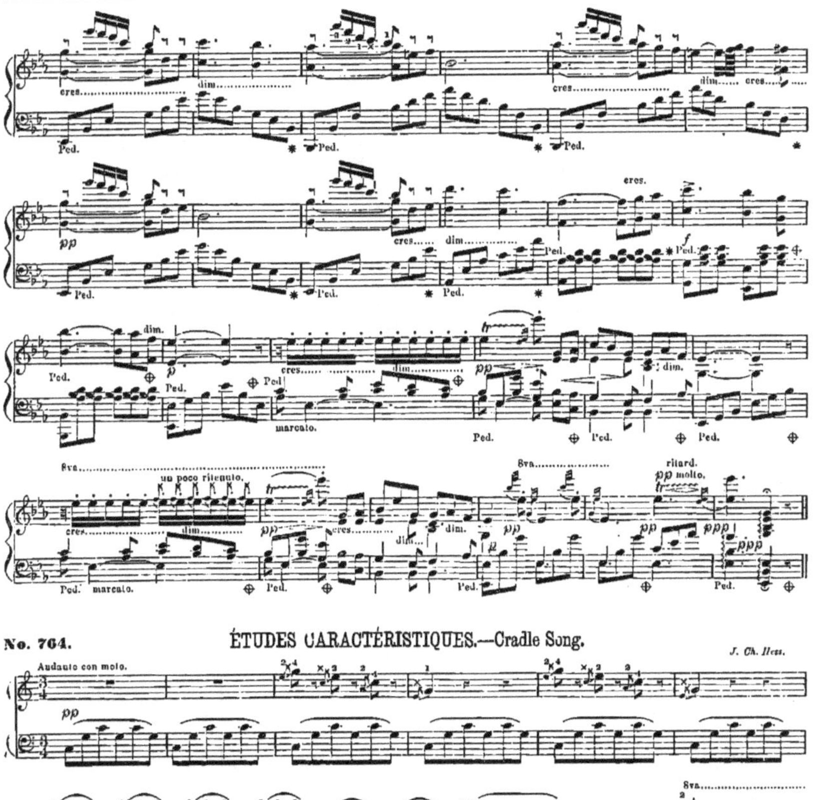


**No. 764.** ÉTUDES CARACTÉRISTIQUES.—Cradle Song.

*J. Ch. Hess.*

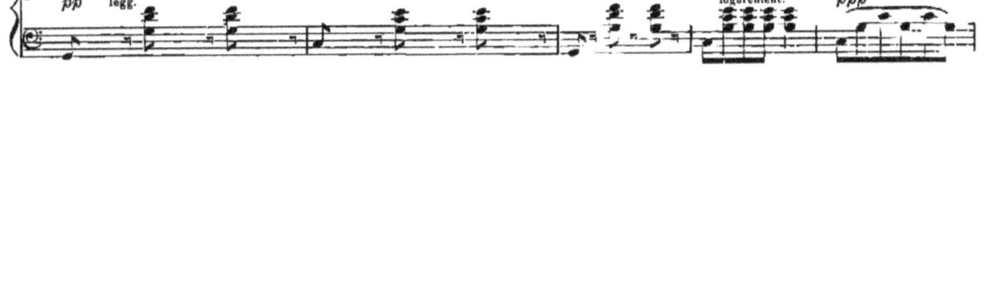

8va
pp
legg.
rall.
p
mf a tempo.
dim.
ppp
risoluto.
L.H.
L.H.
cres.
rall.
cres.
f
sf
grandioso.

Ped.
cres.
Ped.
Ped.
rall.
ff
Ped.
sf p dolce.
legg. il basso.
dim.
rall.
pp legg.
mf
8va
dim.
pp
8va
pp

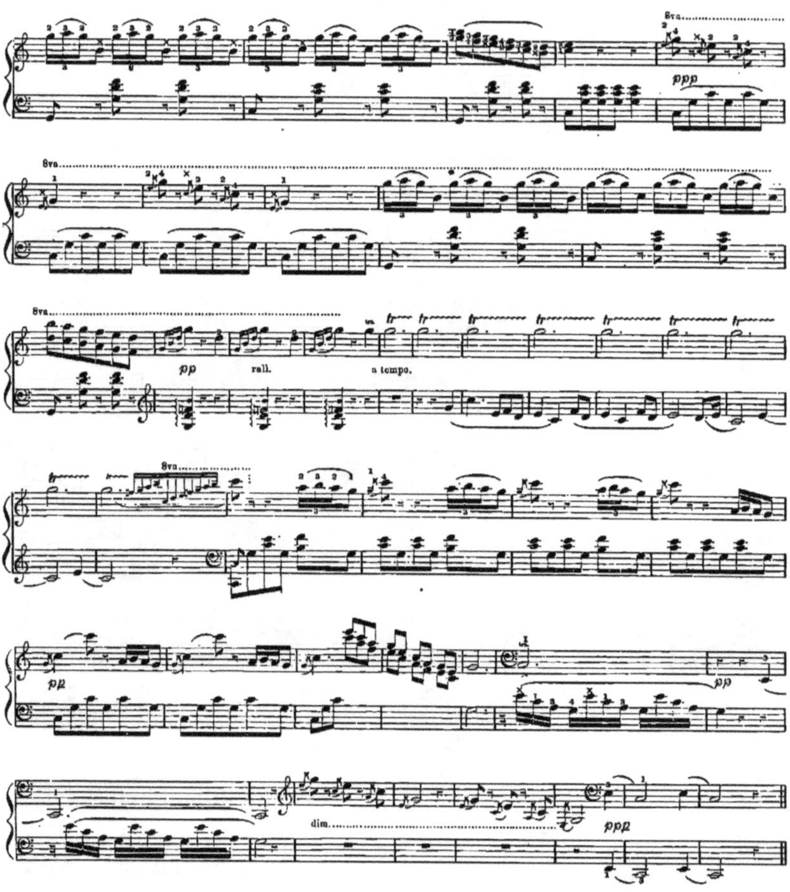
8va
ppp
8va
8va
pp
rall.
a tempo.
8va
pp
pp
dim.
ppp

**No. 765.**

# ÉTUDES CARACTÉRISTIQUES.—Potpourri.

ALLEGRO MAESTOSO.

*A. Baumbach.*

**Russian National Hymn.**

**Comin' thro' the Rye.**
ANDANTE CON MOTO.

**Di Pescatore from "Lucrezia Borgia."**
ANDANTE ESPRESSIVO.

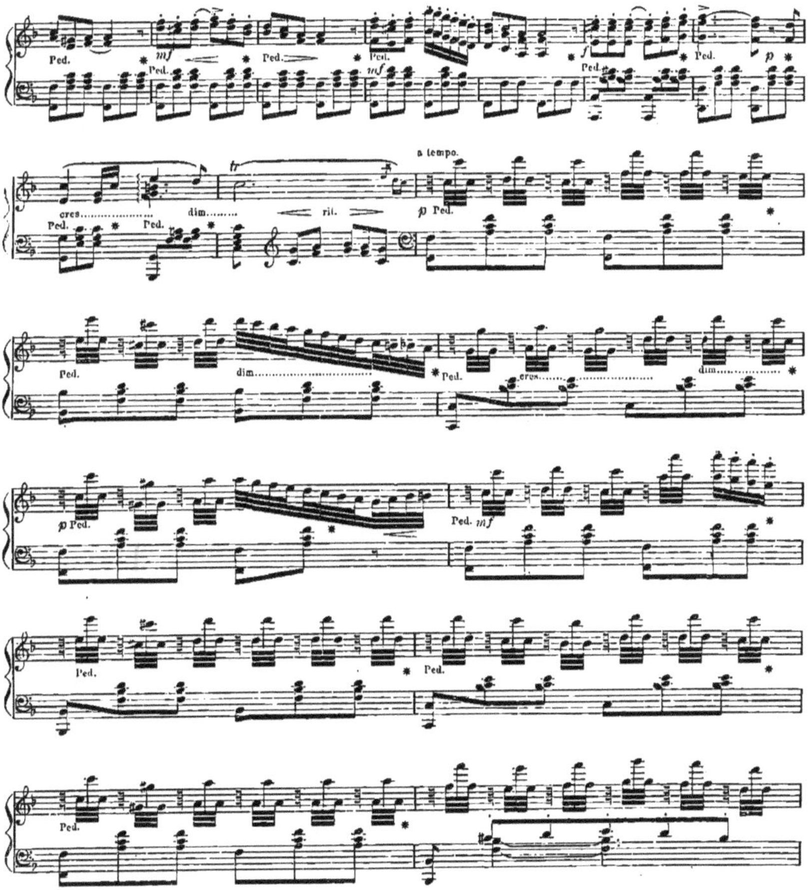
Ped.
mf
cres
dim
rit.
a tempo.
p
f
Ped.

The Battle Cry of Freedom.

ANDANTINO.

Ped.
Ped.
f
Ped.
cres
ff
Ped.
Ped.
Ped. mf
ff
con tutta la forza.
Ped.
Ped.
Ped.
Ped.

# INDEX.